O'NEILL OUTSIDE

PEOPLE AND PLACES ALONG THE WAY

SIXTY-FIVE YEARS IN THE OUTDOORS

By O'Neill Williams

FRANK,

Enjoy.

O'Neill

Dedication:

To my wife, Gail, who steadfastly gave me the encouragement to continue in this little media train and to chronicle my experiences in this book. I'm hoping it can be a bit of encouragement to outdoorsmen everywhere to make the most of their time on the lakes and streams, ponds and forests, and cherish the time spent with partners encountered there.

About the Author
By Dave Altman, Friend and Fishing Buddy

O'Neill Williams

O'Neill told me, "It wasn't meant to be very much, really." He was asked by a marketing fellow once about how far this 'television thing' was going to go. The reply from O'Neill was, "Nowhere beyond the Atlanta area or a few Georgia television stations." That's not exactly how it has turned out so far.

So how does an Emory University graduate, professional bass fisherman and body building champion who once hit over .500 during a high school baseball season end up as one of the nation's most widely known outdoorsmen?

You have to start back during World War II, when O'Neill Williams was born Donald O'Neill Williams Jr. in October 1943. His Mom was a "spunky little hard worker" named Margaret Turpin. Margaret was married to a handsome Army Air Corp Pilot, O'Neill Williams. Williams says both his mother, from Clayton, GA, and his father, who grew up in Spartanburg, SC, were natural athletes.

"Each of my folks worked for AT&T, he in Charlotte and she in Atlanta," said Williams, "They met while corresponding on the teletypewriter and finally ran away and got married in the summer of 1941 on the beach in Jacksonville."

Williams said his parents moved to Charlotte, NC, but it was a short stint, as his Dad volunteered for pilot training for WWII and left for Texas. Six weeks after the new O'Neill was born, Margaret traveled by train to visit Major's Field in Greenville, Texas to let O'Neill see his newly born son before he was to go the South Pacific war theatre.

O'Neill's mother was staying in a boarding house for a few days and her husband was on-duty living in the barracks. They were scheduled for their first afternoon of the three of them together, but good weather meant a day of flying so the meet was cancelled. It turned out to be a dark day for Margaret, as another plane, with engine trouble, crashed into her husband's plane while he waited on the runway for takeoff. O'Neill Sr. was killed instantly. That was 74+ years ago.

Undaunted and undefeated, when O'Neill was three years old in 1946, she luckily found another true WWII hero, H. O. Nash Jr., a veteran of 25 bombing missions over Japan as a radio operator on a B-29.

"H. O. Nash, Jr. is the Father that O'Neill Sr. would have picked out to raise me, had he been able to make the choice," said Williams. "He was a wonderful Dad in every way."

As a 10-year-old, Williams made summer visits with his maternal grandparents to relatives in the North Georgia Mountains. With warm days spent exploring the gentle little creeks below the ridges and the clear, placid lakes dotting the valleys, those grandparents generated in Williams a love of wild places, the critters that live there, and the gentle interaction of nature. O'Neill and his grandparents walked along the railroad tracks to the Tallulah River, and using cane poles rigged with black nylon line, they'd always catch a few little bream and an occasional catfish. It didn't matter. They were together with Williams learning about depression-era times and the lives they had shared.

Williams' step-grandfather, though he certainly wasn't ever considered as 'step', was a Primitive Baptist preacher serving the small congregations in the farming communities around greater

Atlanta and East Georgia. It was with Elder Nash that O'Neill was privileged to angle for catfish from the banks of the ponds owned by a few members in the congregations.

"Granddaddy, also known as 'Elder Nash', took me fishing," said Williams. "He was always decked out in a dark pinstriped vested suit, white shirt and tie and broad brimmed straw hat. I was in a T-shirt and jeans with rolled up cuffs. We must have looked like quite a team to the folks who let us fish in those ponds," he added.

With a row of forked sticks, gathered from the trees close by, holding an arsenal of Zebco 33s fanned out in the shallow water, little O'Neill and his grandfather filled the dark colored ponds with baits of chicken livers and red wigglers. Many a whiskered catfish ended on their stringer and finally at the dinner table.

High school in Atlanta was something different—and Williams made the most of it. Williams excelled at all sports, including baseball, football and wrestling. But after the traditional knee injury forced him out of football for good, he turned his sights to baseball and never looked back. He made the All-State baseball team, and his .567 batting average as a senior is still the all-time record in Georgia High School history. In the middle of that charmed senior season, he was hitting a remarkable .818.

"I still love watching baseball today," said Williams. "It's a much more complex game than many people realize."

But when he wasn't on the diamond, Williams was developing a strong interest in fishing, no doubt spurred by the early days with his grandparents.

"Jeff Hobbins was a high school friend and we used to go to area pay lakes around the county," said Williams. "We'd figured out that baiting a section of the lake with corn for carp and catfish could pay off by allowing us to catch a tub full and then sell them to other fishermen that weren't so lucky," he said smiling. "Here we were a couple of 14-year olds and people would actually 'book' the fish we were about to catch." His friend spent most of his career with Browning and O'Neill on TV and radio. They had clearly developed their business acumen at an early age.

That business savvy that showed in his early teens on the bank of a pay lake was to guide him throughout his career, a gift that he would put to great use throughout his adult life.
Williams moved on to Emory University, where the degree he earned in economics was the second best thing that happened to him: he became reacquainted with a girl from his own high school who would become the love of his life, Gail Williams.

"A fraternity brother of mine had seen a class photo from my high school yearbook and wanted me to set up a date with her," said Williams. "When I called to ask her, she said "I don't do blind dates", so my friend was out of luck."

But Williams was not. "I got up the courage to ask her out on a Friday night and when I saw her again, I thought she was the most beautiful girl I'd ever seen. It's ironic that her maiden name was Williams", he added. Coincidence or good fortune, the two were married three years later and recently celebrated 53 years together, raising two wonderful daughters, Amy and Allison. His granddaughter, Lorrie, is a certified surgical technologist in Athens, Georgia, his oldest grandson, Travis, is the co-host of "O'Neill Outside" Television and Radio, the youngest grandson, Cody, is still in high school.

While O'Neill's career began in the food industry (he worked for Oscar Mayer), his love of the outdoors was building. He competed in many local bass tournaments and won the Georgia Bass Anglers 1979 Tour Championship—and even got some sponsors for his fishing.

But it was in 1982 that his career took off.

"I got a call from Steve Hines, a fellow in the local cable television business," said Williams. "The result was a 15-minute local outdoor interview show called the 'Metro-Channel Sports Fishing Report" with all 60,000 cable subscribers. The truth is that the show probably had about a hundred viewers and most of those were people I called and invited to watch," he laughed.

The TV thing that "wasn't supposed to be much," traveled quite a route. Over the next 36 years, that small cable TV show grew to become "Fishing in Georgia," "Southern Fishing," "Adventures Afield," "Reel Adventures" and finally "O'Neill Outside" and is now in 140,000,000 subscriber households nationally. You can watch it on Pursuit Channel, FOX Sports Southeast, FOX Sports Sun, FOX Sports Arizona and the Hunt Channel.

"We've been honored to build a great audience over a long period of time," said Williams. The show normally delivers a rated weekly audience of over 200,000.

But Williams, whose energy at 74 is still extraordinary, set another challenge for himself.

"I decided I didn't like the shape I was in when I turned 40 so I started weight training and entered the Atlanta Body Building Championship," he said. Always competitive, Williams took third place at age 43, the oldest athlete in the field. "To be honest, it's not like you had to look like Arnold Schwarzenegger, since I was in the 35+-year-old senior division," he said.

But as if fishing, TV and bodybuilding weren't enough Williams decided to take a crack at radio. "I knew that fishermen just can't stop talking, so I thought a radio call-in show just might work," he said. His first job was at Atlanta's WGST in 1990. "That was the home of the Georgia Tech Yellow Jackets and it was well known then, but not as much as WSB Radio. Still, I appreciated the fact that they gave me the chance, and I was making $15 a week broadcasting for two hours on a Sunday afternoon."

Williams and WSB Radio, known for more than 75 years as "The Voice of the South," finally got together in 1992, changed the hours to a 4 a.m. to 6 a.m. timeslot. That show, called "O'Neill Outside," now covers more than 38 states early on Saturday mornings and generates an audience of over 800,000. It will be celebrating 27 years of weekly broadcasts in May of 2018 and the show just may be the #1 outdoor based live radio talk program in the country. "There's really no way to tell," said Williams in characteristic modesty. "It really doesn't matter anyway, but it's flattering that so many similar types of shows have come along in the 25 years we've been on the air with WSB." In July of 2017, Williams added the SB (Sports Broadcast) Nation radio network with 126 affiliates across the nation.

What was "not supposed to be much" has become a broadcast empire that just won't let go; a monthly video Newsletter to 600,000 subscribers, Facebook posts to millions, TV to an audience of 200,000, radio now to 1,200,000, and a website with thousands of daily visitors. He also writes personal columns for Angler, The Outpost Life, Outdoor Unlimited and Dude magazines with a total subscription base of over 600,000.

"The value is having met and worked with quality people along the way, said Williams."

"There are so many that have been a part of our success, including Frank Carter, Jeff Alligood, Dudley McGarity, Ken Sturdivant, Wes Campbell and his family, TJ Stallings, Carol Robinson, Dave Altman, Kevin King, Tom Duncan, James Graves, Glenn Ivie, Paul Smith, Dan Lee, Roddy Sturdivant, Ken Sturdivant, Roscoe Reams, and others too numerous to mention."

O'Neill Williams

Williams says the list could go on and on but the one who always kept the standard the highest, kept the effort maxed and never allowed O'Neill to give up, was the beautiful young girl that refused the blind date but accepted the invitation from O'Neill. "She's my life partner and as pretty as ever," said Williams. In the last 55 years since that first date, Williams said only a very few days have not started and ended circled in diamonds.

I asked O'Neill if he's recognized in public from time to time and he told me this story; "I walked onto a Waffle House early one morning long before sunup and a fellow jumped down from a counter seat and hugged me and told me he loved me and I was his hero.

Flattered but not fooled, I recognized that he just wanted to say something nice, but what he said caused me to think of the true heroes in our lives. I can tell you with absolute certainty that being on television and radio does not make you anything special. Heroes are not rock or movie stars, sports professionals or politicians. No, the heroes in our lives are dedicated people like firefighters, policemen and policewomen, soldiers, nurses, doctors, emergency personnel, teachers and, most of the time, parents. So, I can say without contradiction that, while what I do is a great way to earn a living, it's really "not so much after all."

What Will You Get Out of Reading This Book?

Not all that much really. It's a travel guide to some terrific hunting and fishing destinations, but don't expect an account of which route to take, flight to charter or motel to reserve. No, it certainly is not that, it's simple little stories and recollections about the people I have managed to meet and places I've visited.

It's personal. After all, maybe you have watched a few episodes of our television show over its thirty-seven-year history under various titles as it aired on a number of networks, or, happened to tune in to our radio program early on a Saturday morning. If you have done either, we are friends or sorts. I think of it as an opportunity for me to tell you, to share with you, as outdoorsmen and women, the memories that make up our lives. It's like deer camp or stopping at Bass Pro and running into some friends to exchange stories.

Can it be inspirational? Maybe a little about not giving up or to continue striving for what you want to do or for what you want to accomplish.

More than that, maybe reading this will cause you to cherish recalling your own stories, the adventures and the people that partnered in making those memories golden to you. They are unique to you.

Then too, I tell of a few family members and how fishing and hunting played a role in those relationships. Gosh, wouldn't it be wonderful to go fishing again with your grandfather or grandmother? Maybe you did, and maybe reading about those memories I have raised to conscience can cause you to remember also and appreciate those times.

Anyway, that's enough. Read or listen, however you may, and enjoy if you can. If it inspires your own accounts, write them down, hold them close, share with others and cherish them always.

We have included some outstanding recipes gathered from our years of cooking wild and domestic game and fish from Big Green Egg productions on the television show. Giv'em a try!

Chapter 1: Uncle Ben

O'Neill with Rod and Reel from Uncle Ben

Until I was about 8-years old, when visiting my cousin in North Georgia, all I had to use for fishing was a cane pole. I didn't mind. It had black nylon line; a lead split sinker or two and a small simple straight shank hook. I kept it leaning up against the corner of the back porch next to the well. My cousin, Winifred, and I went fishing every day when we finished his chores; we drew water from the well before breakfast so anyone who wanted could wash their hands and face. This was before a bathroom on the mountainside. We raked the hard packed dirt area around the back steps to give it a fresh look, then fed the chickens and dogs. We 'slopped' the three hogs - that is took what was left over from breakfast along, with a few ears of corn, the pigs were kept in a pen out back beyond the outhouse. The pen had a little tin roof shed so that pigs could get out of the sun. We did that twice a day. The outhouse was a two-holer. We probably visited that only once. Being little boys, we could do that anywhere, and probably did.

Anyway, I liked fishing with that cane pole. My cousin had one just like it. We would catch a Bream or two, sometimes a little Horneyhead, and maybe a catfish from the Tallulah River that ran out of Lake Burton, then through Lake Seed and Lake Rabun and before it formed Tallulah Lake. There was no bridge across the river in getting to the little dirt road to his house, so if the river was low enough and you were driving in the old pickup, you simply 'forded' across the rocky bottom. There was a 'foot log' with a walled up little platform full of big rocks in the middle of the river, where the two logs joined. My cousin and his dad, Paul, had nailed a 2 x 6 on top of the log to give it a flat surface to make the walk much easier. There was a water snake that lived in rocks. We looked for him when we walked the log.

Sometimes we copped a quick glance before he darted away. We'd walk along the railroad tracks that crossed in front of his house for about a mile, then over the railroad trestle that still stood above the river and fished in the deep hole under the tracks. Our bait was red wigglers and an occasional night crawler we dug up from the area around the barn. It was easy for a couple of 9-year old boys to dig up a few. It didn't take long. We'd put them in a Prince Albert tobacco can. I do not recall where the can came from. It might have been his dad's. Seems to me he rolled his own after supper. I remember he would sit on the steps outside the kitchen door, use his Barlow knife and whittle little sharp pointed sticks then toss them aside. There must have been a purpose, but I do not know what that might have been.

I went there for couple of weeks every summer with my grandparents. They were both from the Clayton, Lakemont and Wiley, GA area so the summer visits were a kind of a going home of sorts for them. For my cousin and me, it was playtime every day.

Back to the cane pole; my cousin, Winifred, would keep it handy and did not use it until I returned the next year. It was just like I left it on the porch, in the same spot.

Fast forward to age 10 and with a couple of more summers adding to our adventures. By that time, we'd already graduated to walking the four miles to Lake Rabun and fishing off the steep rocky outcroppings. There I caught my first Warmouth Bream. It looked like an oversize Bluegill with a big mouth. We took it home and cooked it as a supplement for suppertime. My great Aunt Cleo, Winifred's mother, cooked on a wood stove. One of our jobs during the day was to cut kindlin', small pieces of wood, for her to put in the stove fire. Guess everything turned out OK, as I don't ever remember being hungry. No, come to think of it, no matter how much I ate, I was always hungry, but that's another story.

Enough about the cane pole; this story is about my Uncle Ben.

In the fall, around the time of my birthday, when I turned 11, my Uncle Ben came by the house one afternoon. We lived in a little house in Toney Valley, a subdivision in South DeKalb County, and he asked me if I would ride with him to downtown Atlanta and help him pick out a rod and reel. Wow, I was thrilled. We drove down to Sears and Roebuck on Ponce De Leon Avenue across from the old Atlanta Cracker's ballpark. When I was a senior in high school, I played baseball for the state championship in that old park and got a triple on my first at bat. That's another story also. Back to the visit to Sears; we picked out a Ted Williams' model Shakespeare open face reel, a matching rod, spooled it with braided nylon line, a little plastic Old Pal tackle box and even put a few hooks, a box of split sinkers, a red and white plastic clip-on float and one Lazy Ike lure for bass fishing. I was so proud to be able to have a hand in such crucial choices, and was surely grinning ear to ear. Uncle Ben was all fixed up. He'd probably spent $15 all at once on fishing tackle and I was impressed beyond belief, never having witnessed such extravagance before.

We parked in the driveway at my parent's home. The driveway was so short it could only handle two cars at a time. I piled out and ran into the house to show off all Uncle Ben had bought. After the description and viewing all the selections, Uncle Ben fell silent. He'd had the idea all along. Once all the fabulous purchase had been lined up neatly for all to see, he gave it to me.

That was 64-years ago. Uncle Ben is gone now dying on my birthday 7 years ago, but here I am telling the story to you. Why? If that event is so marked in my memory and has for so long and meant so much to a little wide-eyed fisherman, I shout it out again to encourage you to be an Uncle Ben to as many little boys and girls as you can. Take the challenge and follow his lead. Make a little boy or girl happy with an outfit to fish from the bank of a small pond or creek. Maybe they'll write about it one day.

Chapter 2: Date and Brother Go Fishing

Gail and O'Neill at Age 18

It was during my 19th summer that I decided it might be worthwhile to take my younger brother, 11-years old at the time, and my girlfriend of recent vintage out for an evening of fishing. I was an experienced fisherman. Not many guys were at that age. I felt I needed to impress her with my knowledge and aptitude. Okay! Maybe I did not think things through. It turned out to be a learning experience for us all that would foreshadow the future.

I had been catching a few Crappies from around the docks at Norris Lake near Lithonia, Georgia. A short trip, from 7pm to midnight, did not seem too difficult. Knowing about the lake, docks, and general layout would serve us well and we soon located a small 14-foot aluminum boat at the community dock. With lanterns and gear in hand, off we went into the gathering darkness.

Well, first-of-all, my brother lost the only paddle overboard, never to be retrieved. Eleven-year old boys are rarely known for their coordination. However, refusing to give in, I scrounged a lengthy 2x4, about 12-feet long from the shoreline, and I rowed on 'kayak' style, toward a destination not yet realized. That necessary paddling style unfortunately wet the matches in my shirt pocket. That situation unfolded as we reached the designated dock. No matches for the lanterns. What now?

1965 Wedding Departure

Press on; we were there, so fish anyway. As hands and feet scrambled in the darkness on the uneven planks, my tackle box was kicked into the water and floated away. This frazzled 18-year old, trying his best to impress his beautiful date, attempted to decide who should take the blame. Well, it seemed important at the time.
No light, no tackle, little resolve! Give Up! Live to fish another day. Paddle back to the dock.

As I tied a stern line to the post at the dock, I was assured by my date that the bow was likewise secured. The lone female on this little jaunt needed to visit the little girl's room. She and my brother hurried away, privacy and all that. "No problem, you guys go ahead and I'll unload."

It's a Done Deal!

Alone now, I placed the remaining gear on the dock and stepped out. Secured bowline? No, and I quickly did an acrobatic split and plunged into the dark water headfirst. My returning date noticed the soggy footprints on the pavement after I resurfaced and then recalled the part about the bowline. Teenage giggles mounted into infectious laughter as she surveyed the scene.

Gail and O'Neill at Age 42

Remember now these people were only 18-year olds.

There I stood, no glasses, they were lost during the impromptu dive, soaked to the bone, with my dignity dripping wet! Hardly the impressive conclusion I had envisioned.

O'Neill and Gail in 2013

Anyway, we got through that evening, sense of humor finely tuned, knowing a great deal how we would react to and eventually overcome adversity. It was kind of a rehearsal, I guess, that first fishing trip. We are still paddling, that girl and I, sometimes ill equipped, but always willing to go back and start over, with dedicated love and shared humor. We have been together now for 56 years and married for 53.

H. O. Nash

He came back to Georgia in 1946 direct from 25 bombing missions over Japan, as a decorated radio operator on a B-29 crew, the only person in his 20-man radio class to return alive.

He met and married an attractive 25-year old war widow with a 3-year old son.

He had become a husband. Even in later years, he didn't talk much about those 16-hour flights from the captured islands of Tinian and Iwo Jima to Japan and back. The four giant engines roared to life and eight young specialists, barely past their teens, settled in position for the creaking, vibration filled takeoff over a dark Pacific Ocean, not knowing what resistance and terror might await them. As the sluggish propeller driven flying fortress dodged exploding aerial flack, he ignored the cold and fear that must have been a constant companion and focused on the duties that would finish the attack and return the crew safely. It surely took a young man to think of himself as immortal to endure so fearlessly.

The post war years, in the 1940's, were busy raising that youngster and a 2nd son four-years later. In those child-rearing times, the children must have been priority to him, because those two sons always felt they were. Affluent life style; certainly not! Riches? Yes, but of another, more lasting variety.

He had become a father.

You see, 'father' is a word that denoted continuing acts of love, sacrifice, patience, and of enormous responsibility to wife, family and employer, it's not a title.

That little boy, he so willingly accepted responsibility for in 1947, was a busy guy over the formative years, playing baseball, football, basketball, soccer, swim team, diving, wrestling, and even a growing interest in fishing and hunting. You know, in all those years, while not being able to provide instruction for such an array of sports, he never missed a single game or event, not in 15-years of dates and times. He was always there. Not to be the abusive, shouting, sideline parent so often present today, but to simply offer the support to smooth over the failures and rough spots and to give the "atta boys' that would keep his son's effort maxed out and confident.

Yes, he had become a father to me and performed as such for 72 years.

He never missed a day being my father.

Henry Otis Nash at Age 90

Henry Otis Nash died April 17th, 2014, at age 92, and is interred at the Georgia Veteran's Cemetery on the banks of Lake Allatoona in Canton, Ga.

So now go visit or at least telephone your father and tell him you love and appreciate him. I wish I could call mine.

Post Script: Gail gave him the ultimate compliment one day, as he was lying on a hospital bed when his health began its decline, stating to him, "If O'Neill's father could have picked the man to replace him after his death, it would have been you!"

Chapter 3.5: Was This the Start?

Rick with 6+lb Largemouth in March 1971

I was just a regular little kid involved with Little League baseball and the usual stuff but always had enjoyed hunting birds and squirrels with my Red Ryder BB gun and catching bream and an occasional bass in local ponds. For a few summers, until I was twelve or so, I went with my maternal grandmother and grandfather to visit my relatives in the mountains of north Georgia.

There I fished every single day, except Sunday, with my cousin, Winifred. We all went to church on Sunday. He was a kind, gentle, mountain boy, a year older than I was, and was always willing to show the little city kid about the mountains, the fish, and the other critters that live in the hollows and mountain sides. I fished with my paternal grandfather in the ponds around the countryside. I've probably told you and written about those trips many times. You can read about that in another chapter.

I guess the first venture into capitalism, based on outdoor pursuits, occurred when I was 14-years old. See if this works as a start.

I met a fellow in the 9th grade whose name was Jeffery Merrick Hobbins, he went by the name 'Rick'. He was a hunter and fisherman; a good one. I guess his most valuable trait was that his father, Len Hobbins, had a boat and would let me tag along with them to Lake Lanier. But I'm getting ahead of myself. Let's digress to Rick and O'Neill's first commercial fishery.

In the early to mid-50s, in our area of DeKalb County Georgia, existed some of what we called 'dollar' lakes; one could fish all day for a dollar fee and keep whatever you caught. These lakes were very popular, even to the extent that on holidays it was difficult to find a place along the bank to cast a bait. One set of three lakes was called 'Chinchilla' Lakes. Seems the owner had an adjoining Chinchilla raising facility nearby. Anyway, Rick and I went there often on Saturdays and caught our share, nothing special really but we were honing our skills each time. Rick figured out that by putting a half ounce sinker on the end of the line preceded by a rather large treble hook, about two feet above, he could cast out into the shallow upper end of the lakes where the creeks flowed in and could simply rake the hook across the muddy bottom with a jerking motion and snag one catfish after another for as long as we wanted or needed. The fish were there because of the fresh flowing cooler current. Of course, we likely scarred up lots of poor little catfish critters without hauling them in. The lake and land owner caught us and asked us to leave and not come back. We were 14-years old and were not conservationists, so we didn't really understand why the owner was so upset. We do now.

So, by necessity, we changed our weekly summer haunts to a place a few short miles away, which I believe, was called Parker's Pond. Same thing there; catfish and carp and lots of folks fishing on weekends and holidays. Rick and I soon figured out that lake, how to catch the fish that lived in it, and capitalism took charge.

We'd buy several cans of Green Giant whole kernel corn, or another brand since it didn't matter, and toss handfuls out into the lake where we were fishing. A can of corn was priced at nineteen cents so the investment was tiny. The smell of all that corn soon attracted a generous portion of the carp and cats in the pond and we'd be catching them by the buckets full. OK.

So now we thought, let's sell these fish. We certainly can't use them all. Ah Ha! We were in business. On a given Saturday, my mother would take us to the pond about sun rise, and we'd stake out a good spot, and load up the shallow lake bottom with corn. We'd then use corn threaded on our hooks for bait. While Rick staked out our claim and fed the fish, I'd walk around the lake and invite other fishermen to visit with us before the day ended if they needed, and we'd sell to them the fish we had caught. Early in the day, I'd usually get rebuffed rather kindly as in "No sir, don't need any help from you, I'll catch my own" all the way to smartly replying, "I don't need you to catch any fish for me you little punk, get away from here".

However, before the day ended, and his mother came to pick us up as the sun began to drift and the color turned golden, we would have other fishermen standing behind us laying claim to, and offering to pay us for the next catfish or carp we landed. The fee was only $1 to fish, less than that for the corn, and we'd each pocket seven or eight dollars for a day's fishing.
We'd cut forked sticks and line up six rods and reels, usually Zebcos or Johnson Centuries, and fan cast into the area where we'd tossed the corn, sit on our little tackle boxes or simply lie down in the dirt, use our newly found wealth to eat Moon Pies and drink Cokes all day and have profits left over. It really worked. I don't know how we could have been able to tell but we always felt we had most of the fish in the lake right in front of us by noon every day.

Capitalism at its finest. Surely did beat working all day at the local grocery store bagging groceries and making tip money.

Will that serve as a starter for our careers? Rick spent most of his business life as a rep for Browning selling sporting goods all over the world and you know what I've done, and still do, to make ends meet so, what do you think?   It's as good a beginning as any.

During all these years, I guess you could say that Rick and I have been 'selling our catch'.

Post Script:

Rick and I have been friends all these years from 13-year old fishing buddies until the present. He's 76 and I am 75.

OK.

When entered our 30++ years, and our fledging local bass tournament participation began to grow, we were natural but very friendly competitors.

Here goes. Rick called one day and surprised me with the notice that he had been approved to be a 'field tester' for Tom Mann's Jelly Worms, a company out of Eufaula, Alabama. While I was proud for him, I was naturally jealous because I had always thought I was as good a bass fisherman as he and could also be a candidate for association with a bait company.

Notice of Acceptance as AA Field Tester for Creme Lure Company

So, I do not remember how I did it, but I reached out to a local sporting goods sales representative company who sold Creme Worms. It turned out to be the Frank Carter Company located in the Buckhead area of Atlanta. I asked for an appointment and visited with the sales manager, a fellow named Sherman Prather, on a cold January Saturday morning. After a brief chat, he granted me AA Field Tester status. I was so proud. That was the start of a 30-year association involving a vast range of brands and products represented nationally and worldwide, by one of the most powerful and well thought of gentlemen in the sporting goods industry, Mr. Frank Carter. Frank and I became fast friends and, with a story I will tell later, without his help, assistance and advisement, O'Neill would have never had a television or eventually a radio show.

Here's the irony in the story. As far as being a field tester for Tom Mann's Jelly Worms, Rick was only kidding me because he new it would make me envious. When I found out his ruse early on, I intervened on his behalf and the Carter Company also granted him status as a AA Field Tester.

The rest is history as they say.

Chapter 4: How To Take Better Photos

O'Neill Williams - Professionally Done

Photos of days in which you choose to go fishing, hunting, camping or hiking are treasures that actually grow in value with every viewing. Trouble is that most folks do not know how to make the best of it. Here are a few notes and examples of both poorly shot, and properly taken, photos. Are the better ones more valuable? Well, no, but are surely more viewable. If the photo quality and positioning causes you to ask, "Who's that in the picture?" Well, you probably could have done much better.

Ok, here we go. GET CLOSER. I doubt the photo is a landscape shot. Virtually it's a photo of a person or persons, so, GET CLOSE. Understood?

Great Deer Photo but Can't See Hunter's Face

The face should not be covered in shadow. Use the sun or some type of reflector or simply remove or move your cap or hat back on your head to reveal the face. Your face should be centered in the top half of the photo and the bottom of the picture should stop at your belt line. It's easy if you'll just pay attention. It's rarely purposeful to the photo to see your feet, so the bottom is the belt line, center of the top half is the face.

O'Neill with Oklahoma Whitetail

How about a photo of your deer? Wipe off the blood from his nose and mouth, stick the poor critter's tongue back into his mouth or even cut his tongue off and then position yourself behind the antlers. Did I mention to GET CLOSE? Keep that in mind.

Sunset Over the Marsh

Sunrises and sunsets are great topics and it's hard to go wrong. The thing you should do is put a recognizable shape of someone on the trip in the photo. Make it a silhouette if you like, just the person in there. Put the silhouette in a corner with the sunrise or sunset in the center of the top half. This is not hard to do.

Perfect Fishing Photo

I can't say I'm an expert at this at all. Maybe 10% of my photos are correctly accomplished, but we can all do better. I've included a few examples in this effort and maybe will illustrate how to and how not to take photos.

Travis at Sunset – Telling the Whole Story via a Photo

Southern Breakfast

Coffee black, eggs over light or scrambled, biscuits covered in gravy, Swaggerty's Sausage patties, and grits swimming in butter. Sounds like a great breakfast doesn't it? I was in Montana trying for Mule Deer and Antelope a few years ago. That went fine. I enjoyed the adventure. Trouble was I couldn't get any grits up there. They served potatoes. That's a valiant effort, but it wasn't grits and I missed them. I tried to encourage the little restaurant's owner and cook combination to get with the program, but he talked with a bit of a flat accent and couldn't understand my proper English from a guy from Georgia. They all thought I talked funny, although I didn't see anyone laughing.

As a side note, have you hunted or fished in Montana? One thing you might want to remember, the air is free but there's not much of it. It's tough to get enough of it to feel good. Be sure and take a generous supply of Goody's headache powders. If you get one of those altitude headaches, you'll need the powders.

Back to the grits.

Grits has become a fashion statement, of sorts. Is that proper grammar? Is 'grits' singular or plural? Anyway, I had grits with shrimp at a very upscale coastal restaurant on St Simons Island this last week. The grits were (there's that singular/plural problem again) fried in a little square cake with the grilled shrimp on the side. Outstanding! Gail cooked up grits this last week with boiled corn, bacon and little bits of venison sausage. WOW! What we didn't eat, I stored in a little soft plastic bowl for a snack.

I had breakfast with friends in Jonesboro, Georgia last April, I do have a few friends, contrary to popular belief, and the restaurant served little cubed potatoes there, along with grits, of course. Are we losing our focus here? Breakfast around here means grits, not potatoes. We have to decide where we are. Georgia is not a breakfast potato place. Come to think of it, the plate had some orange slices and some green sprigs of some kind on the side. I wasn't impressed and left most of the little garden. What's that all about? Oranges? I drink orange juice sometimes on Sunday. I don't eat oranges for breakfast. If you were brought up around here, you won't either. About 30-years ago, my exploding ego necessitated entering my entrance in the Mr. Atlanta Body Building Championship. It was that 'getting old feeling'. Finished third and wouldn't do it again if guaranteed to win with a $100,000 prize. I almost starved. Lost 40 pounds by eating mountains of oranges, potatoes and pasta. Haven't been able to eat an orange since. I tried one little bite of the green stuff that morning in Jonesboro. I didn't want to look like a complete boob in front of my Yankee friends. I think they are from far and away up north, Raleigh or somewhere like that. The garden didn't taste very good. I'm not sure but that might have been for decorations only.

Trouble is, people who don't like grits don't know how to fix them to eat. Take notes. First of all, you cook grits on the stove. Don't use INSTANT GRITS. You need to get this right. Whatever the cooking instructions say on the box, cook them much longer and just before they're done; add a quarter pound of butter.

How do you eat them? Spoon a giant dob on your plate, add more butter, lots of it, a considerable amount of salt and finally cover them completely with pepper. As a matter of practice, go ahead and cover everything with pepper; eggs, gravy, everything. Mix it all together with your fork in a swirling clockwise motion. If you have grits left over after the eggs are consumed and scattered around your plate, use your biscuit to gather up the remaining grit (grits?). 'Sopping up' is traditional.

Enjoy your breakfast. Following my lead, breakfast as described should last you until lunch with country fried steak, fried apples with cinnamon, mashed potatoes (potatoes are OK for lunch) and plenty of gravy again.

Chapter 6: Cajun Vista Lodge

Cajun Vista Lodge

Every once in a while, yearly at least, save your pennies and grab a destination, a new fishing hole, new tactics, new meals, new life long experiences, and a few new memories. It's an idea whose time has come. Get my point?

Well here's one, one where the fishing's great and perfect to enjoy with your sons, daughters and even dads and moms. Read on. You'll get the idea. This is a good choice for your search.

Cajun Vista Lodge in Barataria, Louisiana, owned and operated by one of the most pleasant, hardworking fellows I've ever met, Theophile Bourgeois. Well, actually, his name is Theophiles Jean Anton Bourgeois III. Cool huh? Instead of reading on, you can check him and his facility out by visiting www.neworleansfishing.com or www.cajunvistalodge.com and those two websites will fill you in completely. However, since you're already into 10% or so of my feeble attempt at communication, stick around a bit. I don't get paid for this, and only do it because it makes me feel important, so do me a favor and read it. If you stop now, you'll hurt my feelings, and I'm sensitive.

O'Neill with a Nice Redfish

Barataria Bay is an hour south of New Orleans and, if so inclined, you can stop there for a stroll down Bourbon Street, but since this is a fishing story, we'll have to handle that subject later.

So, what's at Cajun Vista Lodge? Let's describe it this way; once you park the truck, you'll hang there for a few days and not drive another inch. Three grand meals of ultra-fresh, 'coon-ass' recipes of seafood smothered with Cajun seasoning with Gumbo and smoked sausage on the side enjoyed daily, prepared and served by loving hands, boats manned with experienced smiling guides, completely at home with the locations of myriads of schooling speckled trout and redfish, and finally, comfortable, spacious private bedrooms and baths. Don't stay too long. You'll get completely spoiled. And why not, you only do this once a year or so. The only downside to the whole visit is that you'll have to listen to that whiney Cajun music. It'll get old fast. Tofiel, that's how what we call him is spelled, will change the station, but it won't help, it's on every channel.

Cajun Vista Lodge can accommodate 60 fishermen comfortably. Are you in a hurry to go? I am, and I will be there every October or September with a group of 30 or more. Make your plans now for the fall.

Back to the important part; the fishing.

Ok, here goes. Barataria Bay is inside what it called 'the marsh', otherwise known at the Atchafalaya Basin, a 30-mile wide, 90-mile long stretch of rich fertile water full of grass, lily pads, canals, all 4 feet deep with millions of Speckled Trout and Redfish. The 'marsh' is the direction and route that the Mississippi wants to flow but the river has been managed by some very smart people to go to New Orleans via giant berms. It's all about economics, and I understand that. We can't let New Orleans dry up, after all, remember Mardi Gras? As an illustration of the amount of catchable trout, the legal limit is 25 per day per person and, by lunchtime, daily, the boat, with three to five fishermen, will have a limit, 75 to 125 trout. Really! Why so great? For the last ten centuries or so, the Mississippi River has been dumping fertile water into the 'marsh' from the Midwest and the fish population enjoys it. It's a giant 'nursery/hatchery' for game critters.

Theophile and a Couple of Friends

How about the Reds? Wow! Put on a Road Runner with a plastic trailer or a shrimp tipped jig under a Thunder Chicken casting cork, cast to a cut, or creek branch filtering from a grass line and hang on. You'll have another limit before lunchtime, and then go back out. The Reds are big, healthy, strong, hungry, brightly colored and living there by the millions, ready to break your light leader, bend your rod, and make you smile heartily. If it helps with the struggle, know that you'll probably be eating the rascal red that night after he's spent a few minutes on the Big Green Egg, and he's served to you with Cajun Rice and hot sauce and, if you've been nice, and so inclined, a cold beer.

Theophile with a Big Red on Flyout Trip

I'm including a few photos to whet your appetite for such a trip. It's only about seven pleasantly driven hours from the Atlanta area and totally worth the expense and effort. The downside is that you will be totally spoiled and desirous to returning monthly which, I might add, you can do because the season is 12-months long. If you like, and haven't already made plans, be in touch with me, O'Neill, via my Facebook page (@oneilloutside) or website or call directly to Cajun Vista and speak to Josie, and come along with us. It's a group of guys from here and there that I call the "Deeply Disturbed Fishermen." The dates are in September or October. Travis and I will be there to exchange stories about each day's adventure.

Chapter 7: Henry (Hank the Yank) Cowen

Henry (Hank the Yank) Cowen

We bounced around from cove to cove, peering as quietly as possible into the flat water where the little creeks fed the great lake. The shad were there all right, flashing first left then right, sometimes breaking the surface veil as the predators loomed underneath. Just what was it that forced the activity, bass or stripers? We hoped it was stripers.

Today Henry Cowan, a New York Yankee on our Southern Lakes, and I are searching the up-lake waters of Lake Lanier for Striped Bass. Interesting isn't it that a Striper is a true Bass but a Bass is a Sunfish. Anyway, this fly-fishing stuff is a bit new to me, however, since this is my first attempt to catch on of these line-sided champions on a fly. I have often thought little of this fly-rod business; usually concluding that one could do better with conventional tackle and buck-tails, plastic jigs, and top-water baits. Today I am the student.

Henry, a thrice-weekly visitor to Lanier and an accomplished fisherman with a fly rod on waters all along the East Coast from Maine to Florida, has rigged for me an eight-weight rod spooled with intermediate line. A 'Henry's Easy-Cast', a fly he ties himself, adorns the 10-pound tippet. A few minutes of false casting are required for me to even approach a decent presentation. Rudimentary success arrives with his hands on instructions, and I am ready to threaten the sleek predators of the coves.

Henry relates that yearly in waters like Lanier, Clarks Hill, Hartwell, Carter's, Allatoona and many others in the Southeast, when the late winter or early spring surface temperature hit 53 to 60, striped bass will streak into the coves and gingerly pick off meals of threadfin shad. The trouble with conventional tackle during this special time is that with the shad being so small, usually not over 2 inches in length, the baits are necessarily too large and the stripers ignore them. A fly, however, is perfect.

Hank with a Nice Striped Bass

Well, after a few hours of fanning the foggy air above the surface, I am a believer. By lunch, Henry and I have landed 9 gamesters, with the largest just under 12 pounds. And what a treat, the largest took my fly in not more than 18 inches of water. I saw the hungry fish approach and strike. I am here to tell you that stripers will take a fly when larger baits will fail.

Good grief, what a task ahead, now I will have to buy more rods and reels. Maybe you should try it too? A visit to the tackle shop may be in your future.

Chapter 8: The Number One Best Bass Fishing Lake in the World

Late Afternoon at Kingfisher

Wow, what a title; the best in the world? You be the judge. Let me tell you about it.

www.kingfishersociety.com. Sound familiar? Here goes. 115 acres of cypress filled black water in Laurel Hill, NC, owned and operated by Jim Morgan and managed by him and his family for the last 150 years.

I could give you all the particulars about its origin back to the civil war and all that, but you can read as much on its history as you like on the Internet. That's not the point.

T. J. Stallings, one of the kingpins at Tru-Turn Hooks and Road Runner Lures, recommended King Fisher Lake to me for television show. He knows his stuff, and I trusted him on this location and its fruits without the slightest reservation.

I was there one Fall day to shoot an O'Neill Outside television show, so thought I'd spend a few minutes in the boat with Jim to get our discussion started, what I'd like to cover in the show, you know, just get our communication on the way so the show would move smoothly. It's better when you talk with someone for a while, you know what they mean and establish the more relaxed feeling that friends have when they've fished together a while. Responses like "what?, when? and huh?" do not translate reliable information.

It was two o'clock in the afternoon. With daylight saving time in place, I didn't think we'd really get into any fish until 4 or so, and thought we'd have at least 2 hours to get acquainted. The cameraman came along just to get some 'beauty' shots of the lake and surrounding landscape until I anticipated the bass would start biting.

By four that afternoon, Jim and I had already caught and released 20 largemouth bass between 2 and 6 pounds. Yes, you heard me, about 60 to 80 pounds. None were below 2 pounds, and no giants over 6. The show was completed, and it has aired several times on "O'Neill Outside" Television.

O'Neill with a Typical Catch Made Daily

Get my drift?

On the second visit during a cold February day, the air temperature was 24 degrees and the water temperature was 42. Cold! I thought, what the heck, let's give it a try. Anywhere else, it would be a day that you claimed you had a bite, but truly didn't. I had recruited Davy Hite, sponsored, as I am, by Buckeye Lures, designers and manufactures of the Mop Jig. That's the lure we were using and is a great 'big bass' bait. As you read this, you must take into consideration that Davy has won the Bassmaster Classic, has been awarded Bass Angler of the Year and is a consummate pro. OK? Not your average afternoon fishing buddy.

In three hours that afternoon, with me in the front of the boat and Davy at the stern, under those conditions, WE caught 7 Largemouth Bass that totaled well over 35 pounds. OK, Davy caught 5 and I caught 2 which is about right since he's at least 150% better than I am but, never-the-less, the lake produced them.

I've been to King Fisher Society now 6 times. Largest bass? 8 pounds. Most bass in one day; we had 50 between 4 and 6. I took Travis to Kingfisher too. A photo is included in my narrative. That bass was 19 inches long, 18 and ½ inches in girth and weighed in at 8 pounds and 9 ounces. Travis caught him on a Mop Jig of course.

Travis with 8 lb. 9 oz. Largemouth

Like to catch Blue Gill, not hybrids, Blue Gill? The lake record is 3 pounds and 5 ounces but that's a story for another day.

Oh, too, you don't have to bring your boat, no. Jim has 20-foot Stratos bass boats with electric motors, the lodge will accommodate your party and a gourmet dinner is provided. Only four fishermen per day are allowed on the lake.

Am I kidding? It's the bass fishing trip of a lifetime at the best bass fishing lake in the world. www.kingfishersociety.com. Read about it and go. I'll see you there one spring day.

Chapter 9: Choose Your Poison

Possibly for you and certainly for me, those wonderful days that I've spent fishing and hunting are much more memorable than being in the audience for other sporting events. I mean think about it, while a football or baseball game is certainly memorable, being in the woods or on the water as an actual participant is bound to hold more permanently in your memory than watching either on sight or on the tube. These days can be recalled with great fondness for the rest of your life, well maybe fondly, maybe not.

Let's try a few easy ones, whatcha' say? How about coldest, hottest and wettest? Think about that while I write/talk.

For me, the coldest fishing and ultimately one of the wettest and most dangerous was during a March bass tournament at Lake Sinclair near Milledgeville, Georgia. I had thought that the shallow stained waters in the back of a creek far from the colder river flow might produce so I motored into a sheltered area in the back of a place called Potato Creek. The water temperature was 45 degrees, the air 33. It was cloudy, windy day with sleet on the way for the evening. In a word, it was brutal for a day of fishing.

Back then, the middle 70s, most of us that thought of ourselves a being more professional, did not use pedal controlled trolling motors, we just stood on one foot and, by placing the other on top of the trolling motor, controlled the direction and speed of the motor that way. Of course, that way of standing went away when I had to have my right knee replaced a few years later. Anyway, the wind was blowing me along, the trolling motor hit a stump abruptly stopping the boat's direction and I just tipped over into the frigid water from my amateurish stand. I was all alone, dressed in a zip-up thermal winter cold suit, stocking hat the heavy insulated boots, and had just launched myself right over the side head first. The water wasn't deep and I could stand on my toes and keep my round little face above the surface, but believe me, I quickly got soaked to the bone, my clothes soaking up the frigid water like a sponge. I pulled myself up over the side of the still rocking boat and sat for a second and tried to figure out what to do. Nothing came to mind other than just getting dry and warm. Surprised? I idled out of the shallow waters and positioned to make a quick run back to the dock and eventually dry clothes. On the way back though, it got interesting. With the air swirling around me during the 5-mile trip, I got really cold and started seeing things; imagined birds, dark objects and other non-descript flying things. Back at the dock, a couple of other fishermen helped me get the boat out and I drove to the motel room to warm up. Incidentally, in the tournament the next day, I didn't catch a single bass. 93 boats, 186 contestants, entered and one guy caught two Bass and won everything. Boy was I cold.

The coldest time hunting occurred when in Canada up close to the Northwest Territories. We were shooting an "O'Neill Outside" show for Whitetails. My cameraman was Scott Sawyers, never a complainer, a true tough guy, more about that later. Anyway, we hunted three days. The high temperature was 1 degree above 0, the low every morning was 18 to 22 degrees below 0 and we had to drive a four-wheeler 22 miles in the dark to get to the stand which was a pop up tent on a wooded platform about 12 feet above the ground. The wind blew a dry snow in on us and we were covered having to dust it off occasionally. We had to put those plastic kidney-warming patches on the camera to keep it from freezing. In that part of Canada in December, I think, the days are short, so the hunters stay in the stand all day and try to eat sandwiches but they were frozen by 8 am. Cold enough?

How about your hottest day afield? For me, it was a blistering hot opening day of the Whitetail Deer season in South Carolina, August 15th as I recall. South Carolina has the first to open and longest running Whitetail season in the country. My cameraman, Jeff Alligood, and I were in one of those summer heat waves across the South; high pressure, no wind, still, and scorching hot. We were shooting a television show that needed to air in a few weeks so I couldn't put it off any longer. About 2 in the afternoon, dressed in full camo and facing an open field of fescue, I sat on a little tree-stand and watched a brilliant ball of fire settle ever so slowly. Six and one-half hours it took. The Whitetails were hot too, napping most of the day and had quite obviously turned nocturnal. I never saw a living thing move. I found out later the high temperature that day was 102 degrees. Boy was I hot.

And what about the wettest from rain? Going for shark off Amelia Island one gray first of September day, Captain Jimmy Johnson and I anchored up over a likely spot, a deep hold about 200 yards off the shoreline at Fort Frederica in the Amelia River. Jimmy is an outrageously successful fisherman. Doesn't matter what species you're after; kings, tarpon, shark, redfish. Jimmy can catch 'em. I guess we should have checked the weather more closely, but Jimmy and I feed off each other's enthusiasm, one more confident than the other and are not easily deterred. Well, a hurricane decided to stop for a few hours before venturing inland across Georgia. We were in an open boat and endured/fished for 7 hours and got pounded by 12 inches of rain; 12 inches. OK, no one had the sense to give up and go in. After all, we were really on some big ones up to and including a 275-pounder. Jimmy had 'em located. Boy was I wet.

Have you a story or two? Bet you do. If you can find someone to listen, you'll enjoy the telling. I just did.

Mark Scores Again!

The strike is almost gentle in its first few seconds, but when the fish feels the slightest resistance, up he comes, streaking to his full height above the glistening surface shaking his head in the futile effort to rid himself of the intruding pressure. Indeed, it's so quickly done, the strike and first jump, that I am hardly grasping the heavy rod before he cartwheels again and strips thirty yards of heavy line from the reel. By the time I have belted the rod butt and leaned against the pull, he has raced another hundred feet, grey-hounding up and down wild and frightened.

Mark Releasing Another 100-Pounder

The first twenty minutes rushes by so fast, I hardly remember my shouts. But Mark smiles brightly and laughs at my ravings. His sky blue eyes see this action daily in the summer months. The second third of the first hour begins to grind my knees into the gunwale and the fish bears down trying for deeper water. As we both become weary of our fight, the gallant warrior wallows a shallow trough twenty feet across the stern, his thick body half out of the green water. A half-dollar size eye looks blankly in my direction.

Both of us, the Tarpon and I, cry for relief as the hour passes and this champion of the flats yields to the lip gaff. Mark calmly guesses him to be at 135 pounds. The waves lap against the boat as Mark revives the heavy beast and says good-bye. The tarpon slides away into the gloom.

Tarpon are like that; scary, brutish, sleek, fast, and with a 1-2 punch worthy of a heavyweight. Some have said the tarpon are God's perfect game fish. I agree and these are the reasons why I think so; tarpon will take surface baits, deep baits, cut baits, the fly, live baits, they bite early, late, summer, winter, they weigh in at 100 pound average, jump dozens of times and then you get them to the boat, there's nothing to do except let 'em go. When you catch your first, take lots of photos and measurements and get a fiberglass replica made for your trophy room. It's less expensive and then too you don't have to kill the fish. When I am ready for another fight with a gamester that will play by the rules, it will be with one of Mark Noble's summer buddies, one of his friends. He has plenty of playmates in the shallow waters of Georgia's Golden Isles.

Contact Mark Noble at www.georgiafishing.net/

Chapter 11: Mountain Trout and Holiday School Days

Abby Jackson with a Nice Trout

With the holidays in full swing in November and December and the kids out of school so much of the time, I have a couple of your days planned out for you. It's all easy once a gracious person like myself sets in to help. If you and your wily children like to trout fish, try the delayed harvest sections of the Chattahoochee or Amicalola Rivers, maybe Smith Creek in North Georgia. In whatever state you live, the choices for trout fishing are endless. Even if your children don't like to trout fish, take them and check to see if they do. All are outstanding streams, chock full of rainbows, browns and a few brookies. These pristine waters are part of your state DNR's catch and release program.

Those streams are micro managed by the DNR to hold lots of gamy little critters and you can catch a bunch. I recently fished the Chattahoochee below the Palisades inside the perimeter just north of the Atlanta city limits and caught all I could stand. The clear clean water where I was standing was only about 18 inches deep, which made for easy wading, an abundance of fish and lots of fun. I'll bet the kids would love it. The rules are to use artificial bait and a single barbless hook. Round up some equipment, some wide-eyed kids and get started. It'd sure be better for them to be wading in the gently flowing current of a trout pool than sitting at home playing computer games and then they'd have something good to talk about at school when they get back that none of their friends would. It would make them feel special. The Amicalola River is a mountain stream in north Georgia and has lots of space for camping so make a weekend of it if you like. I'll bet there are several in your state, in the fall, when mild temperatures and the leaf colors abound.

Everyone likes to have a story to tell and now, after fishing these places, catching lots of rainbows, being the center of attention and taking many photos and camping along the river, they will too. I guarantee, they'll tell about this adventure over and over and over again and again all of their lives. I do it all the time.

So, what about the child who never has done any fishing and really has no desire to go? I say trick 'em. Tell them to dress warm and get ready for a surprise. I can practically guarantee satisfaction when the first trout is brought to the net. If they're afraid of the current, put them on the bank and cast from there. Fail to yield. Few are born with the desire to go fishing. They have to be taught through experience. Very few aren't hooked after a short time on a fish bank.

What's in it for you as a parent? Beyond the obvious, it's fall and the brilliant colors abound all across Georgia and the Southeast, November at Amicalola and December along the Chattahoochee. It will be so refreshing to see the colors the abundant forests provide. Beats the office no matter how accommodating.

Finally, this is not a team sport. You've probably involved your girls and guys in soccer, little league baseball and maybe football too and that's all very good, but this little trip is one of individuality. It's you and her or you and him. It's not about the team winning or losing, it's just you, and in doing this, you win every time.

When it's all over, you have a partner for life, you've planted a seed that may grow into a life-long wholesome sport and finally your children spent the day alone with you, their father. Today, regrettably, that's sort of hard to come by.

I'd like to add a footnote to this column I penned many years ago by offering to you that the best mountain stream in Georgia and probably the East coast is the Soque River near Clarksville, and the best outfitter on the river is Blackhawk Fly Fishing. You should look at the Blackhawk site, www.blackhawkflyfishing.com, and plan on going. Now be assured this is not a child's trout stream, not because of any difficulty in fishing or wading but for the size of the trout. On several occasions there with friends, both relative amateurs and seasoned veterans, results would dictate to me that this just may be the best trout stream in the East.

Blackhawk is catch and release only, and you must have a guide they will provide. The guide is there to help care for the trout, all of whom are captured in a photo, if you like, then released without being taken from the water. The average catch is 10 rainbows in the 20 to 24-inch range and an occasional Brown up to 28 to 30 inches before lunchtime. Only two fishermen can be on the river at a time. Wait a moment. I didn't hear a gasp from you when you read the average catch number and size. 10 bows over 20 inches and browns in the territory of 28. Now, you can gasp. It's true. My guests and I have been witness to it many times.

See? The Soque is a bucket list stream for trout fishermen.

From the Blackhawk site: www.blackhawkflyfishing.com/press-video/

The Soque exits Blue Ridge Lake and crosses private property making the stream manageable by the owners. That's how Blackhawk has cultivated their mile of stream into its championship form.

One of the features of a visit is lunch. Abby Jackson is a foodie, publishes a magazine reflecting that expert level of interest and is a gracious host for both the stream fishing and dinner. The magazine is www.southernfarmandgarden.com/

So, make plans and go.

Chapter 12: The Tennessee River, Wilson Dam and Brian Barton

55 lb. Blue Catfish

Sheffield, Alabama is easy to find. From my cabin in North Georgia, it seems all one has to do is drive to Chattanooga and follow the Tennessee River through Alabama and you'll end up in Sheffield. That's good. North Alabama is dominated by the Tennessee. Every town and multiple bridges all lead along the river to Sheffield and beyond.

But I'm slow in getting to my story.

Brian Barton and I had been trying to schedule a fishing trip to the river for some years, but have always gotten waylaid somehow by rain, storms or what not. This time it came together. Jeff Alligood, my show cameraman, editor and all-round partner for the last 25 years, and I drove over on an early morning in October and located Brian at the dock and ramp, about a mile downstream from Wilson Dam, which holds back Wheeler Lake and pushes fertile waters down into Pickwick Lake.

Fall's declining seasonal temperatures invite billions of baitfish upstream from Pickwick Lake to the hard surfaces of the dam to spawn. Wilson Dam is a huge structure belching water that is full of baitfish, and a variety of gamesters that I've never witnessed before in fresh water. You have to see it to believe it.

Get this picture; Brian operates a perfectly adapted War Eagle fishing boat for these waters. It's large, spacious and all set up for boating large fish in large numbers. You do not want to try this the first few times on your own. You need Brian.

The bait? Threadfin and Gizzard that Brian has already caught. Tackle, relatively light line, say 10 or 12, a small split shot and a Tru-Turn red light wire hook.

Method? Brian navigates the boat to a special rocky flat behind the dam and we toss the live baits along the edge of the current and allow them to sink among the boulders that are huge car size dark shadows in the current. Then just hold on.

40 lb. Striper

What do you catch? First of all, you get bit every cast, yes, every cast. Brian and I fished along the flat up against the dam and downstream less than 100 yards. In an hour or so, we caught Largemouth Bass up to four pounds, Smallmouth Bass to six, Channel Cats to three pounds, Black Drum up to 12 or so, hooked and lost stripers and/or giant Blue Cats up to, I'm guessing here, sixteen to thirty pounds that we simply could not get out of the rocks, and even some very respectable two plus pound White Bass. Many of his clients have boated blues to 70 pounds, Largemouth to 12, Garfish to 5 feet, White Bass upwards to 4 and drum to 40 pounds.

Brian fished for about an hour after we left that day. He had caught a six-pound Smallmouth and sent me the photo.

Twin 6 lb. Smallmouth Bass

Brian has a constant stream of clients, with many making lifetime catches.

Do you have to be an experienced tactician and angler? Not really, a rank amateur or child will get his string stretched dozens of times in short order. I guarantee that if you have Brian and two anglers, someone will have a fish on the line all the time. It's almost impossible to describe.

There's not much else to say. Tell you what, look at the photos and use your imagination. Contact Brian and ask him to get the War Eagle ready because you're on the way over.

For contact information and a host of photos of giant catfish, stripers, bass and drum, your anticipated catch of the day, find Brian at www.brianbartonoutdoors.com

Travis with 25 lb. Rooster

We decided we would head south. I mean it's already spring and winter has been a long time going, so we planned a very special trip a few years ago. Way south.

Costa Rica.

Crocodile Bay Lodge/Resort; look it up, may be the best overall fishing in the world for a combination of saltwater big-game species. We routinely catch and release ten to twelve Sails a day in the 100-pound category. My largest was 130+ pounds and took at least 90 minutes to boat, Roosters, the fish with the racing stripes that is, up to 40 pounds or so, my very first Rooster weighed it at 75 pounds and nearly broke my back, Red Snapper, Bonita, Sierra Mackerel and the like. The food is excellent, accommodations lush, clean and safe. Crocodile Bay is a pretty nice place.

You gotta want to go there. It'll take a Delta flight from Atlanta to San Jose, Costa Rica, limos everywhere for a stay overnight near the airport, and a forty-minute charter to the lodge. Don't worry. These guys are experts executing the arrangements, travel, rooming, etc. without a single hitch. O'Neill has visited a dozen or so times. So how much does it cost?

I'll tell you in a minute, but first, the equipment. Thirty-three to thirty-eight foot Strikes, Whaler Outrages, dozens of other sea worthy craft, staffed with friendly, efficient, English speaking captains and mates, all take your anticipated mystery out of the day. I truly believe that Crocodile Bay Resort is the best-equipped location in Central America. Turns out, it's a fisherman's dream trip.

You really don't have to take anything. Computers are in the lobby with high-speed Internet connections, ample and appropriate clothing available in the local shop should you be purchasing very special shirts with Crocodile Bay Resort logos, toiletries and what not. Did I mention the food? OH, my goodness, chefs roam the kitchens preparing a feast three times daily. It's a treat. Often a portion of your day's catch is your centerpiece for the evening meal. You will have to purchase or bring a bathing suit for the pool with swim up bar, and the hot tub atop a raised platform to view the sunset.

Did I mention also the eco-tours, waterfalls, horseback riding and zip lining? The fishing can wear you out so there's plenty to do otherwise in making this trip one of a kind. Then too, a world-class spa is only 20 steps away, available for evening massages and facials.

Let's get back to the fishing. Travis and I traveled there a few years ago and during one of the days offshore, we raised thirty-four sails and caught seventeen. What a day! Inshore the next day we caught Roosters to thirty pounds and Red Snapper in the upper teens. What a day! I said that already didn't I?

Anyway, how much does it cost? About $2,000 for three days I suppose.

Should you go and when; yes, late December, January, February, March and even April while the turkey season is in full bloom and the truly great bass fishing across the South has kicked in.

Just go to www.crodocilebaylodge.comand find out all the particulars.

Chapter 14: A Date with a Friend

I held the thermos cup with both hands trying to warm up a bit. The steam zipped over the rim and vanished in the dry air. 22 degrees! The trees were bare and boney and the tops whipped back and forth in the wind against a steel gray sky. I knew it wasn't a good idea to drink coffee from the stand, but I was freezing. The so-called sub-zero boots evidently had miscalculated the temperature. By now my ears were crimson, chin numb and eyes watery. What a day and not a deer in sight.

It's December at 6:15 pm and I could be home with Gail eating country-fried steak with mashed potatoes, some fried okra, a big glass of iced tea and golden biscuits covered with butter and gravy. Fresh lemon pie would follow. Instead, I'm sitting on a crude stool in an old homemade wooden stand with a weathered canvas top. My back is to the wind blowing back into the piney woods and I'm vainly looking for the buck I've glimpsed on three other occasions. He's a prize. I've seen him only fleetingly; a rack held high above the brush, a rump disappearing in the darkness, the thick body quickly crossing a firebreak. He doesn't stand still long.

A grizzled old doe walks underneath me and nervously munches on what's left of the clover and wheat stems. I perk up a bit but remain still and silent. After a few moments she drifts up to stare directly at me, eye to eye. So much for the scent shield I liberally sprayed around.

I heard nothing, but her head snaps around and ears cup forward. She's heard or smelled something in the clear cut up the hill. In my frozen state, without movement, she dismissed me as being no threat. She stepped forward, raised her slender neck and sampled the air. I looked in the same direction trying to detect an antler or tail or leg; some motion. Was my buck there? The doe knew. I didn't.

After a long, frozen moment, she quick-stepped into a thick patch of oak saplings off to the right and vanished. To be a herding animal, Whitetail surely do spend a lot of time alone.

Nothing! Thirty minutes later, a bitterly cold darkness enveloped my surroundings and I stiffly climbed down. Getting colder by the minute. At about 200 yards, my yellow beam of light picked up the heavy prints. There in the muddy roadway, my buck had crossed. The huge tracks said he had stopped and stood there. Was he looking at me? But I had scanned so hard for him. How could he have avoided my watchful pose?

Oh, well, hopefully he's still near the hillside and without a single thought of me, he's visiting the scrape lines he made in the leaves from under the overhanging limbs and marking his territory, with his heavy antlers, he's rubbing the small trunks bare along the paths and, as the temperatures drift downward with the falling leaves, he'll sometimes look to the edge of the small clearing for movement. Someday soon, in the waning light of an early winter afternoon, he may see an old friend. I'll be waiting and appreciating him and his talent for staying alive.

Chapter 15: Jimmy Johnson, Amelia Island, Florida

Captain Jimmy Johnson

Topping the crest of the last bridge to the island, the lazy, skyward reach of the purging smoke from the towering mill stacks to my left, assured a calm, easy, fishing day ahead.

Looking east into the growing light, I knew Jimmy would be ready. He is always ready, anxious, almost gleeful and smiling. The fish wait.

I met Jimmy Johnson some years ago during my first visit to Amelia Island seeking King Mackerel from the spotty but fertile live coral reefs a few miles offshore. That was a very successful first hand partnership. Since then, I have caught giant Amberjack exceeding 60 pounds, Sharks from the Amelia River spawning areas topping 200 pounds, Tarpon, Spanish Mackerel, Reds, and Trout. Jimmy is a good guide. Amelia Island is a good place.

Located only a few minutes from the Jacksonville, Florida airport, and lying at the junction of the Georgia and Florida coasts, fed by the Amelia and St. Mary's Rivers, Amelia Island is a worthy destination for the fishing sportsman.

Gently sweeping easterly, rising and falling with the changing tides, the rivers provide the highway for your quest. Inshore, roaming schools of Redfish root along the sandy flats always eager for a well-presented fly, hopping plastic jig, or live shrimp. Toothy, slender and hungry, spotted Sea Trout migrate over and around the oyster bars with the tides. Live shrimp and artificial lures will readily trick a tasty limit.

Before the river leads off shore, we are obliged to pause and drop cut bait, on heavy tackle, into the deep, 70-foot deep holes, where a myriad of Sharks set up housekeeping. The remains of historic Fort Clinch stand to the right, squat and dark, along the rocky beach, observing our efforts. The sands provide a pleasurable base for vacationing families less than 100 yards from our shark den. The Amelia and St. Mary's Rivers are America's East coast's largest spawning area for a multitude of shark species. On many occasions, Jimmy and I have hauled 150 to 250-pound sharks from the deep, cool current. Black Tips, Bulls, Nurse, they are all heavy and strong.

Now heading into the sunrise and bounding over the light chop, Jimmy and I search the horizon for the sea birds that, with sharp vision and effortless track, will direct us to the game species that round out the full slate of possibilities available from Amelia. Dolphins, Kings, Wahoo, Tuna, all plentiful to a full-time guide like Jimmy Johnson.

Jimmy is knowledgeable, enthusiastic, eager, energetic; all readily obvious by the bounce in his step and the results of his fishing forays. Jimmy and I have fished together on a dozen or more trips. He has never failed to deliver. On both King Mackerel and Giant Barracuda, one 40-pounder jumping 20 feet over the bimini top of his boat, we have harvested our fill when neighboring boats went empty and wanting.

Chapter 16: Okeechobee Adventure.

Okeechobee Catch

It is a bit hard to describe, but here goes. It's an inland 500,000 acre freshwater sea covering 660 square miles, shaped like a dish, averaging 7 feet deep filled with hyacinth, bulrushes, hydrilla, and the like, and it's perfect for what may be the largest single concentration of Largemouth Bass in the world. Favorable temperatures for Largemouth Bass growth and spawning, an abundance of food, minimal sport fishing pressure, considering its size, and lastly a reputation everyone tries to cherish and even elevate, makes Clewiston, Florida's Lake Okeechobee the necessary destination for every fisherman. Indeed, if you are a bass fisherman, you must go to Okeechobee. It is like a pilgrimage.

During my last trip in early April, to the "Big O", as most anglers call it, our party of 8 caught and released over 150 quality Bass in a day and half up to 8 and ¾ pounds, with many in the 5 to 7-pound range. These came on an array of baits from plastic worms, to native shiners, to top-water chuggers. We fished with guides arranged by the marina. Art, Dan, Jerry, and Eddie are all seasoned guides with dozens of years of experience at their command. They will take care of you with new equipment, boats, food, bait, and success that comes with daily exposure to the lake and what it offers. You'll start early and fish until 2 or so in the afternoon, returning to the marina for refreshments at the Tiki Bar, a little rest, and supper at nearby restaurant. What a deal!

Your cool ride will begin on the rim canal, a deeply dredged circular passage that collars most of the lake. Most boaters use the canal to travel to the different areas. It is along the edges of the canal that you are most likely to see the Okeechobee's oldest and crustiest residents, giant Alligators, sometimes reaching 10 or more feet in length. Out in the lake, noticeably large White Pelicans lazily sail overhead and look down in a disapproving way. These are Pelicans that reside only on Okeechobee, are exclusively freshwater feeders and are 2 or 3 times larger than the common Pelican that you see so much of around saltwater. In the early hours, ospreys soar and dive, soar and dive, over and over, in their lonely pursuits and nervous gulls squawk their presence and occasionally sweep in to grab your discarded baits. Coots chirp loudly as they paddle among the weeds, always seeking and never seeming to find.

But what you are there for is the catch, the swirl, the strike, and the opportunity to bag your career Bass. Each cast holds the promise, indeed the likelihood, that it is this one or the next effort that will bring your prize. But if it does not, and you are disappointed, just remember where you are and what the adventure is that you truly seek. I think you will find that in just being there on Okeechobee is sweet enough.

Dan Dannenmueller

It's warming up fast and the Crappie are biting. Up the rivers at West Point, Sinclair, Oconee, in Southern lakes and reservoirs across the entire South all the way into Texas, the time is right for you to get in gear and round up the tastiest little fish in Southern waters. Well, maybe a Walleye is better, but not by much. Anyway, there are lots more crappie available than Walleye. In Georgia the daily limit is 35, I believe, so that's an indication that there are plenty to be had for all.

As an example to be applied to most of the southern reservoirs, if you'll just motor up any major river that feeds the lake, like the Oconee River above the I-20 Bridge and turn right into the main river and follow the mobs of boats, you'll just naturally round up with a cooler full of scrappy Crappie. Remember, the waters are still cold, so move slowly, give the critters lots of colors to choose from and before you know it, you'll be an expert perch jerker.

O'Neill and a February Crappie

Have you seen the really tricked out crappie rigs? I have one friend in Alabama, well actually more than one, but a few. He is a perch jerker supreme and has a fully rigged Ranger all set for Crappie fishing. It's impossible to describe but I'll betray a confidence here and tell you that he paid $78,000 for it. OK, he was a friend and now you see why. I don't have to trailer my simple little rig to Alabama to fish for Springtime Crappie. He has it all. Multiple rod holders out front of the bow and behind the engine, long willow branch rods with soft ultra-lite tips fashioned with super light line and tiny little multi-colored Road Runners. I have to tell you, it's really impressive. He says the key is to move ultra-slowly. Early season Crappies are slow to bite, but they will. To my surprise, he also says that once they spook a bit and stop biting, go elsewhere for a few minutes and return for another half dozen or more. Keep a cooler with ice instead of just your live well. They clean up better and taste better by doing that.

Never mind those high and mighty bass boys in their 'quick start' boats that you'll see flying up and down the lake. They're fast and famous, but take heart in the knowledge that during dinner soon, while you're enjoying some sweet tasting fillets, that bass jumper will be washing that expensive personality extension.

O'Neill and Another Slab Crappie

Since those days of fishing off the docks as described, the Crappie fisherman has become sophisticate with hugely expensive rigs, tournaments well attended with the anglers becoming famous and recognizable. One such very successful fisherman and a pioneer in the category is Dan Dannenmueller. Like so many of these fishermen and competitors, he has customized his Ranger with 10 rod holders on the bow fitted with 10-foot soft tipped rods, multi-stationed electronics and a generous portion of patience in his soul.

The result is a Crappie Tournament Competitor of excellent repute and success. He gently and closely ranges the spring and fall reservoirs in the relatively shallow waters, locates the giant schools of tasty Crappie and rakes them in by the buckets full. The next time you spy a custom wrapped truck and matching trailer marching to the lake, take note that it's very possibly not a bass angler but a highly equipped rig completely devoted to denting the millions of schooled up black and white Crappie in the local reservoir.

Chapter 18: Old Stories

Ah, these good old outdoors stories, recounts of fishing and hunting days afield. Stacked like leaves of gold to be turned again and again, shared with and amplified to an eager audience.

Sure, Ernest Hemingway, in novels, and Russell Annabel, in magazine tales and books, and many other writers chronicle their adventures for your reading enjoyment. However, those stories are their stories, not experiences. No personal story exists like one from the outdoors.

For instance, it was a bright, clear, windless November day, about lunchtime, in the Lewis Pond area on Lake Seminole, way down in Southwest Georgia. Tom and Jim were in the boat beside us, about 400 yards from the nearest shoreline. Along with the tasty sandwiches and ice-cold drinks, the topic of conversation was to find out why the dark waters had been giving up so few Bass. We'd been working hard on it.

The banter came to a halt as I looked over my shoulder to see a six-foot long (aren't they all six feet long?) rattlesnake tracking his way directly to my old boat. The rust colored menace was closing the space between us rather rapidly. Mr. 'No-Shoulders' was on his way. As he peeked over the transom, looking, it seemed, directly at me, I tapped him on the head with the longest rod I had. He retreated, coiled and rattled, sitting high in the water like it was a solid rest. We left.

I passed along the day's exciting occurrences to the nearby bait shop owner that night. We were told that rattlesnakes could not and would not swim. I guess I must have been dreaming, but I have the pictures. Oh well, it made for a great story. See what I mean? They get better with age. That happened fifty years ago.

One of those surprise March ice storms was on the way, and I was alone pre-fishing at Lake Sinclair before a Sport Bass Anglers tournament. Sinclair is in south central Georgia and not known for ice storms and such. As the skies darkened and wind whipped the water frothy, I was back in the shallow forty-four (44) degree waters of Potato Creek, slow rolling a spinner bait along a stumpy flat. The trolling motor whined, gurgled and splashed as the high wind tossed the bow up and down. Back then, it wasn't the norm to have a foot-controlled trolling motor. Most of us just stood on one foot and placed the other on top of the unit and controlled it that way. On the downward descent of a wind-blown wave, the motor shaft slammed down on the top of a stump. I lost my balance and fell out of the boat. Think about it, there I was, up to my chest, snow mobile cold suit and heavy boots rapidly soaking up the freezing, muddy water. The tolling motor was still running and taking the boat away from me. Luckily, I managed to grab the circle tie-down with my finger as the boat started to swing away.

After muscling up over the back next to the motor using the prop as a step, and sloshing forward to the bow, I felt surprisingly warm and was tempted to stay on and fish a little while longer. Sensibilities prevailed, so I started the long run back down to the Little River ramp about three miles distant, to take the boat out and dry off. As the thirty-three (33) degree air swirled around me, my body temperature fell rapidly, and I quickly became delirious, dodging imaginary birds and other dark objects passing overhead. Hypothermia? Maybe! Although thick tongued and colored light blue for a while, I recovered promptly with no apparent damage, at least my fishing partners didn't make fun of me very long.

That little adventure happened over forty-five (45) years ago.

Then there was the time....well, you get the idea. Outdoor stories, unique and personal, can be told and retold, passed along by loved ones to loved ones, and possibly, after many years have waned and after you have long since gone, provide a connection to you as you lived your life.

All set? Inspired?

Chapter 19: Randy Smith

Randy Smith with Sponsor Patches Proudly Displayed

He was the best tournament bass fisherman I ever knew, and when a fully rigged bass boat was to be awarded as first prize, you could almost always bet that Randy would be standing with the winner's trophy and the ignition key in hand.

Charles Randy Smith was born in Manchester, Georgia and made the waters of Eufaula, West Point, and Barletts Ferry, in Southwest Georgia, his own, and became famous for his catches and tournament wins. We met in the mid 70's. I had entered in a regional bass tournament at Barletts Ferry one spring.

Informed by some of the local fishermen to whom I had talked, that my best finish could only be 2nd place no matter what I brought to the weigh-in stand, because of this Smith guy, meeting him became a priority. I made it a point to do so after the final weight in. Oh, by the way, Randy finished 1st, well ahead of the other one hundred and thirty fishermen, O'Neill 29th.

Anyway, he was small, lean, friendly and weathered with sky-blue eyes and slightly bowed legs and topped the scales at about one hundred and fifty pounds over a 5'9" frame. He would have been taller except for those legs.

Over the next few months and years, we became friends and fishing partners, traveling the local circuit, building up time on the lakes and searching for recognition and sponsorships.

I have never seen anyone as sharp as Randy with spinner baits or with top water plugs. He was a master. The list of his victories is too lengthy to chronicle here, but I know he won at least six bass boats and several state championships during his career. He overflowed with confidence, was deliberate, prepared, and could always seem to "figure 'em out." He once weighed in an incredible twelve bass catch in a single day tournament at Eufaula that tipped the scales at just over eighty-eight pounds, a 7.33-pound average, with a twelve pound kicker. Think about it. Please recall that in the 70s, the daily tournament limit was twelve bass over twelve inches in length.

Randy was a storyteller, recounting fishing and hunting adventures well into the night. It was always a delight to hear his thick, country southern drawl. Descriptions were colorful and filled with characters unique to his imagination. Were the stories true? Don't know, but he entertained us all with the telling.

But Randy carried more than heavy stringers. Vietnam had been in his history when we first met and had been kept at bay but eventually came to the forefront during most of our trips in the last few years of his life. The memories of firefights, intense combat and deaths of companions had opened the jungles in his mind and they had become dense and dark. Alcohol smoothed the dreams and clouded his memory but made him bothersome and misdirected. He lost his job and soon most of his friends, fading listlessly into despair and loneliness.

It was in 1995 that the single car accident took his life. His jeep left the road in a curve near Clarks Hill Lake in East Georgia where he then lived. Thankfully, he was alone. It would have meant a lot to him that he had hurt no one. When he died at 48 years, we put all his worldly possessions in the trunk of a relative's car. Seems a shame, doesn't it? All the dozens of trophies and smiling, heroic first place photos had long since gone.

Randy Smith Died in 1995

Randy's demons, shouldered back from Vietnam so long ago, had finally worn him down. It took over 25 years, but they finally got him, a decorated war hero and my fishing buddy. I still miss him.

Chapter 20: Nicknames. Got One?

Nicknames! Aren't they great? Whether you're a fisherman, hunter, gym rat, sports fanatic, baseball or football player, even a golfer, nicknames serve us well. It's a guy thing, I believe. After all, I rarely hear of a woman giving or calling another woman by a nickname unless it's quite obviously a compliment. Of course, I could be wrong about this.

Anyway, nicknames bridge a communication gap. Using a nickname you've heard or have personally bestowed on somebody usually is much easier to remember, and is almost always a great deal more descriptive as to the personality, physical attributes or talents of the named.

Let's take a look at a few. I'll bet you can think of dozens. For instance, a guy who works out with us at the gym every morning I named 'Frog'. I don't know his real name and doubt if the other guys there know it either, but it's very descriptive. I started calling him that after we saw him kick his legs when trying a heavy lift on the bench. He really looked stupid and the leg kicking didn't help a bit. The name fits him perfectly. He's now 'Frog' to everyone in the gym and always will be.

A fishing guide at Lake Lanier is friendly, cooperative, never raises his voice or gets upset, and is really a nicer person to us than we deserve. We call him 'Sweet Milk'. Need I say more? I don't think he minds. Fits him well doesn't it?

A fellow I got to know recently races stock cars on Saturday night at a track in Jefferson, Georgia. He has a great record of wins, yet we call him 'Crash'. See what I mean? I wouldn't remember his given name as well.

Our youngest daughter, Allison, was 'active' let's say during diaper changes, baths, and such as a baby. Her older sister, Amy, called her 'Twister'. Allison is now stuck with it. Our grandchildren, Travis and Lorrie, her nephew and niece, now call her "Aunt Twister."

There's 'Monkey Man' at the gym, he has long arms and short legs. That was easy wasn't it? Another is called 'Stuff'. Don't know why and don't think I want to know. I had a fraternity brother at Emory nicknamed 'Stump". He was short and well, you can guess the rest.

Famous and infamous college and professional athletes carry a myriad of nicknames. Some fit, some do not. "Homerun Baker" from the old major leagues hit one home run, I think, then never another. "The Babe" name had nothing to do with a Baby Ruth candy bar and the origination is unknown according to Sports Illustrated. The Babe was known, of course, for home runs but started his career as an excellent pitcher. Pro Footballer, Dick 'Night Train' Lane, got his nickname because he was afraid to fly so took the night train to away games. Think about it. Jack Nicklaus was "Ohio Fats" being rather plump and from Ohio. Pro golfer, "Champagne Tony Lima" was called that for obvious reasons. He liked the stuff.

Funny isn't it that the Largemouth Bass is not a bass but a member of the Sunfish family like a Bream. A Striper is a bass.

Of course, too, nicknames abound that seemingly have no obvious connection to reality. A fisherman I recall that competed in local tournaments was called 'Coot'. That's a water bird. Don't ask me, I don't know, maybe he's known for being good at fishing in shallow waters. Another very good fishing buddy was called 'The Rattler'. I could speculate on that but won't just now.

I could go on and on and usually do, but by now you want to ask, my nickname is ….. Are you kidding? You'll have to ask someone else, and then I'll still deny it.

Chapter 21: The Start of Radio

O'Neill at WGST in 1990

Having been airing on television with shows of various names as it grew from the 15-minute long "MetroChannel Sports Fishing Report" to ones more traditionally televised as "Reel Adventures", "Adventures Afield" and finally "O'Neill Outside" as it grew, I had come to know that fishermen just couldn't stop talking. "Where'd you guys go last time, what did you catch, when you going again, etc.?

Following that realization, I though an outdoor based live radio talk show could be popular.

There were two prominent AM radio stations in Atlanta, WGST and WSB. I located the names of the program directors and began telephoning and asking for the opportunity to pitch my idea. WSB would not return my calls and, I have to tell you that if you don't return my call, it wasn't one you failed to return, it was twenty calls not returned. I hate to give up. I had thought the existence of my TV show and a minor reputation and popularity in that arena would get an appointment. It didn't from WSB.

The program director at WGST, Eric Sidel, did return my call and we met one summer mid-week afternoon at his office in the Buckhead section of North Atlanta. Eric was a very pleasant and friendly fellow who had given Neil Boortz and Clark Howard their radio show starts, so many years ago, with each eventually enshrined as members of the Radio Hall of Fame. He listened to my idea and said he would check into the possible popularity of such and to call him back in a couple of weeks. I did. He said he had evaluated the idea again with his staff and decided that there wasn't enough interest in the subject. My response was, "You're wrong" and informed him that I'd give him a chance to change his mind. I called for another meeting later. He said he had not changed his mind, but I could visit anyway. Did I say he was a friendly and accommodating fellow? When I arrived a week later, he looked at me over his glasses, clasped his hands together on top of his desk, smiled, then threw up his hands and said, "I give up, you can have Sunday afternoon from 5PM to 7PM." I would call it "The Great Outdoor Show".

Gail and O'Neill

Gail and I traveled downtown every Sunday afternoon and produced the show. It was summer with lengthy days so the signal from WGST was still strong and we did OK. After sundown, WGST was one of the stations that the signal drops to a whisper.

The deal was that we were to receive a share of the monies from advertisers. After a few weeks, we had one sponsor, Georgia Power Company, that was sold by the WGST sales department, from which, our share was to be $15 per week, which we spent stopping weekly at The Varsity for hot dogs, hamburgers, and fried apple pies. A few of my friends challenged the wisdom of doing all that for $15, but Gail and I thought differently.

The trouble in getting any money from advertising sales was that the sales staff at WGST wouldn't try and sell it, because it really would not get much interest or money at that time of day on Sundays, but they didn't want me to be 'out there' trying to sell it and be representing WGST. Result was poor revenue.

We slugged on.

After the show became noticeable to the outdoorsmen and women around greater Atlanta, WSB started their own outdoor show with a very popular TV weatherman hosting and inviting guests into the studio. It was a recorded show so, in my judgment, it would not work as well as ours and it soon floundered for whatever reason and was discontinued. I listened a few times and it was good but now it was gone. Too bad, there was plenty of room for both of us. Believe me, you must truly want to do this. It's not easy. In the meantime, I had met a fellow named Neil Williamson, who was soon to be a stalwart college sports personality and broadcaster at WSB for the next three decades and still is. He arranged for us to have a two-hour slot at WSB. After fifteen months at WGST, still making only $15 per week, we started at show at WSB, in 1993, on Friday nights from 8PM to 10PM, airing on the Bulldog Radio Network, a collection of affiliates that broadcasted the University of Georgia football games among other programs. The show was still called 'The Great Outdoor Show'. It was winter and I recall slopping into the studio at Peachtree and West Peachtree streets through cold rain splashing the puddles in the old WSB parking lot in the dark holding a fist full of subject notes. After a few months, Neil talked the new program director into giving us the Saturday 4AM to 6AM slot on the WSB signal that, at that time of day, covered 38 eastern states and still does. The bonus was that WSB would let me sell advertising space in the show and I could keep 30%. Yee Haa! We worked hard at selling it and connected many of my television advertisers and sponsors to the radio show. Remember the doubting and second-guessing I'd gotten from friends about starting at $15 per week on WGST? In short order and working hard at it, Gail and I were making over 50 times that per week. So, it goes.

O'Neill During the Radio Show at WSB

Every Friday night, or actually every Saturday morning, we'd get up at 2:30AM and drive downtown to WSB. In 1994, at 50-years old, we could do that and stay awake for the balance of the day, so the weekends were still OK. Gail began going with me to WSB for the show, so we both would be on the same time schedule for those Saturdays, and she soon started screening the calls and getting her own segments and sponsors. She always wants to help. Now, in 2018, in our mid-70s, we must go back to bed for a couple of hours after the show. Since we have lived in the north Georgia mountains since August of 2015, almost a two-hour drive downtown to WSB, we would arise at 2:00AM, drive downtown and get back home at 8AM. It was a six-hour effort. Since then, with the engineering skills applied by our webmaster and 'do everything' friend and employee, Houston, we've outfitted our little cabin with the necessary Internet connections, computers and transmission gear to send the show to WSB remotely. I'll tell you more about 'Houston' in another chapter. Instead of six hours, it's two and one-half hours, then we can go back to sleep for a little while.

In the spring of 2017, I read a press release announcing that BassMaster Radio was to begin airing on the SB (Sports Broadcasting) Nation Radio at 6AM to 7AM Eastern to 126 affiliated stations nationally. Excellent! BassMaster is a recorded interview style show from Alabama and a good one. We looked at the SB Nation schedule and saw that the 4AM To 6AM time slot was merely a re-broadcasted recorded sports talk show about professional and college teams.

I made the call and offered the idea to SB Nation Radio to air "O'Neill Outside" live on Saturdays. Just in case, some time before, at my request, WSB had given me the syndication rights to our show as it airs there or anywhere else for that matter. The fellow in charge of SB Nation programming, Matt Perrault, liked the idea and we started airing Saturday mornings on the SB Nation Radio in July of 2017. 'Houston' then connected us via live television transmission to Facebook and low and behold, we were simulcast on WSB, the SB Nation and on live TV.

What a journey. We now receive live calls weekly from fishermen and hunters from Texas to New York to Florida and occasionally other countries while listening on their iPhones, iPads and/or computers.

What started out in 1991 as a 'begged for' appointment at a local radio station, based on a subject that was rejected as not worthy, has turned into the #1 live outdoor based radio talk show in the world with a weekly live audience of over 1,000,000.

Don't ever give up.

Chapter 22: Shoal Bass

Excellent Shoalie

It was just a very pleasant trip. It was a hot summer day ahead, but the water was cool as it made its way down river from the dam. The pull of the paddles was easy and rhythmic and silent except for the water drippings at the finish of every stroke. We rose up high in our seats to see the first set of shoals, knowing that the first bites from the little fighters would not be far away. Shoal bass are like that, grayish green with stumpy bodies just full of fight. The world record is only about 8 pounds or so. Do not worry though; they make up for being a bit short by being aggressive and fearless. I know some people like that, O'Neill included.

The Ocmulgee River exits Jackson Lake in central Georgia and quickly makes an about face from summer's boating, skiing, and crowds. Gentle, quiet, private, indeed almost lonesome in its journey south, this river harbors a target for the fisherman most prized, the Shoal Bass.

My fishing buddy, Glenn, and I are veteran fisherman. Glenn is retired from Georgia Power and an excellent angler. In this case, Glenn is more the tutor and I am the student. However, surly we have harvested enough finny rascals from southeastern waters to make us a bit jaded as to what is a sporty goal. That is why we both really enjoy this river and its chunky bass. Using small crank baits, spinner baits and an occasional plastic worm on light tackle, we catch and release twenty-five or so of the little fighters in half a day. From a canoe, and wading the shallow rock filled cascades, one can be close to the action. It feels new every time. I recommend it most highly for a departure from the regular reservoir and pond routine. On your first trip, it will take more time than you think. Each pool, next to the thousands of rocks and wood, looks like it will hold bass. Take it from me, you cannot get to every one on the first try.

I am told the upper Chattahoochee holds Shoal Bass. I know the Flint River does. I have not had a chance to try either, but I will just bet I do soon, maybe in the fall before the first frost.

Chapter 23: Hawgs in Texas

O'Neill with Georgia Hog and CVA Muzzleloader

The hour had already pushed the warm Texas sun westerly, giving us a dusty, golden look down the narrow clearing among the trees and brush. Dudley glassed the dark hump 300 yards distant. "It's a boar and a big one," he said in a low voice. Funny how, when you're in the field or woods with game sighted, you'll drop the tone of your voice, sometimes to a whisper. Must be a natural instinct. Dudley McGarity, a center fire rifle and muzzleloader company president and top-notch hunter and tracker from Atlanta, and I had traveled deep into South Texas to extract a respectable wild hog or two from the gnarly tangles of Mesquite. I intended to take one with a Muzzleloader. For my money and time, hunting wild hogs is infinitely more fun and productive than a great many other outdoor pursuits. Besides the resulting Bar-B-Que is worthwhile.

Dudley is a seasoned hunter having bagged large game from Florida to Alaska, Whitetails to Caribou, Rio Grand Turkeys to Black Bear. To have a classic stalk ready to take place made his eyes light up, his mind kicked into gear and a half smile flashed across his face. He was really looking forward to what we had before us. His modern equipment betrays him or else he could pass as a long-range hunter during the early years of the exploration of our country. Had he a 'possibles' bag, powder horn, skin hat, long beard, hatchet, flint lock and fringed coat-sleeves and pants, you'd be seeing a throw back to the early 1800's.

A warm afternoon breeze gently pushed at our backs. We knew we couldn't expect to execute a direct stalk. We'd get winded for sure. The robust old veteran just down the path had lived his many years by being cautious and aware of danger. Dudley called for a wide swing north and then angle back south to intersect the trail upwind from the wily critter. Sounded like a cool idea to me so I followed a few paces behind, my short legs pumping to keep up with what looked to be a leisurely pace to my companion. The undergrowth was high and thick and pulled at our boots and gear. Low slung Mesquite branches plucked at our hats, and steeply banked dry washes appeared from nowhere and angled off into the flat terrain, sweeping right then left then disappearing. Up and down we pushed hard for a half-hour or more kicking up a Whitetail or two along the way.

Quietly now we crawled up to the grassy edge of the pig trail and glassed down toward where the brute was first sighted from the opposite direction. We'd made it. The fragrant Texas air wafted into our faces. We only had a few minutes until the fading light would make a long shot ill advised. Three younger boars had joined the boss and were acting out among themselves as to who was number two in the clan. Number one, standing off to one side, tall and aloof, paid them no attention, taking a relaxed moment to scratch his backside on a fallen oak trunk. We could hear the rough bark scraping against the course black hair. He grunted with delight.

Good! We'd made the most of our time. Only thing was, could we go undiscovered and take a reliable shot with so many noses ready to sniff us out? The .50 caliber CVA would be more than adequate up to 150 yards or so, but I wanted to be inside a hundred. I was readied with a .50 caliber Accura with a Konus 3 x 10 x 44 scope, two 50-grain and one 30-grain totaling 130 grains of magnum power to hurl a 290-grain PowerBelt Bullet. The knock down potential was there. All I had to do was relax and make the shot and the stalk would be worth it.

We waited.

Armed with speed loaders, a practiced muzzle loading hunter can be ready for a 2nd follow-up shot in about 10 seconds. I prefer to view that as an emergency tactic only and place myself heartily into the one-shot challenge that black powder hunting affords. That's a challenge I accept. Muzzle loading should be viewed much like archery but with much greater range; think close, choose your camo carefully, practice stealth, cover your scent, and finally stalk, if you can. To be a successful muzzleloader advocate, you must be a better woodsman and hunter. I like the idea.

All North American game species can be taken with a modern muzzle loading rifle. The new PowerBelt Bullets, available in hollow point, AeroTip, .45 and .50 caliber are true big game takers offering reliable performance and dependability. Whitetail, Mulies, Elk, Pronghorn, Moose, Black and Brown Bear, Sheep, Goats; all have been taken by the black powder enthusiast.

Today's hunt is no different. Although the hog, down the road, now only 80 yards away, weighs in at 200 plus with hulking back and scarred forequarters, he can be taken with a delicate shot no differently than with any high-powered rifle.

Shadows reach out to us and cross the quartet just ahead. We were losing precious light, and in a few moments our shot. We get a break. One of the youngsters had made the big guy mad with a sound or movement unknown to us. He lumbered a few yards out into full view to swat the offending adolescent with a roundhouse head butt. A noticeable 'thunk' filtered through the trees. The resulting high-pitched squeal pierced the air and I raised the CVA to my shoulder.

The huge black herd boar, thick and muscular, stood stock still as if to let the group survey his bulk. He was fearless and proud and respected as the enforcer of the sounder. I released the safety, slowly exhaled and sent the huge bullet home just behind the left shoulder. At 80 yards it really packed a wallop. We heard it clearly. He tried to sprint to the right, away from the direction of his fleeing brethren. In only 10 yards or so his forelegs collapsed, and he pitched forward and died.

The size of these wild pigs is always surprising to me. Up close they are long, tall and heavy bodied. We were very fortunate to have this wary specimen venture out so early in the day as most of his activity would be during the half-light of early morning and late evening. For the old singular boars like this, the afternoon hours are usually passed well hidden in the cooler shadowed wallows under low, thick brush, completely protected from potential danger.

Some landowners consider the wild hog to be a very undesirable addition to the wildlife community. From their view, hogs could be detrimental to the landscape in many circumstances. As a hunter who exclusively uses a CVA muzzleloader for rifle hunting, I find this big game animal to be a formidable quest.

Travis and Giant Hog After Extended Stalk

I'd like to include a brief account of the time Travis stalked a true giant of a hog. Travis is very particular about his hunting. He rarely ever takes a bow or muzzleloader shot beyond 30 yards. It's a thing with him. The photo of Travis with a high sign of completion occurred in East Georgia on dairy property owned by a good friend. Travis and his cameraman and fellow hunter stalked this sounder for two hours trying to pick out the boss boar and it truly paid off. Wind conditions must have been perfect for them to pull it off. The hog in the photo weighed in at over 450 and was as brutish as they can get and was, in body shape, as close to a true razor back with the tall shoulders and upward curving snout as one can imagine seeing in the East.

Giant 51-Pound Redfish.

Are you a Bass guy? Bet you are. I am too. Ever caught a 51-pounder or, for that matter, many or any over 10 pounds? Very few folks have, although many think they have, but that's another subject for another column I have in mind. I've been promoting a new horizon for the Largemouth Bass angler and have said so many times during our show productions. What's that new horizon?   Inshore Saltwater. This time, permit me to circle around a single 'finny' critter, the magnificent Redfish, and point you to two destinations where you can get it done and with whom. Just thought of another, so it's really three.

First, let's talk about the fish and what to expect. The World Record is 94 pounds, caught many years ago somewhere off the North Carolina coast, I think. OK, enough about that. You're not going to catch a new world record, just a few for the adventure, and for the grill. The guy is dumb as a rock, he can be spooked and still will bite, is always hungry, is a survivor, grows rapidly, eats plastics, spinner baits, crankbaits, can be spotted in the shallows and is a target for casts and, finally, a fabulous table fish.

My largest is 51-pounds and I've included a photo from my trophy room. It's a fiberglass replica, of course, because we weighed the fish and put him or her back to make other Redfish to catch later. I don't care if it's only a model; I just wanted you to see it. I was fishing in the Banana River near Cocoa Beach and saw this giant at the head of a school in about 2-feet of water against the lightly colored sandy bottom. I casted a small curly tail jig on 12-pound test line and he took it. After the hook set, the fish swam past the boat pulling the whole school along with him and my fabulous guide, Shawn Foster, also known as Doctor Drum (Cocoa Beach, Florida, Phone: 321-784-0094), shouted, "That's a 50 pounder!" It weighed 51-pounds. Ok, enough about me, what about you?

Let me direct you to three target destinations and the people who will act as your host.

O'Neill and Another Redfish

Spring! Theophile Bourgeois and the Cajun Vista Lodge. You'll be bunked in private rooms in a fabulous 100-year-old renovated school house, Theophile can easily accommodate over sixty guests, the meals are always a fresh fish banquet with gumbo and Cajun dishes, you'll walk to the boats only 30-yards away, partner with seasoned, experienced guides and cast to thousands of redfish spread out across what may be the best inshore, light tackle saltwater fishing in the world. Located in Barataria, Louisiana, Theophile operates the most comfortable and productive destination on the Gulf Coast that I have ever visited. Using Bass fishing weight tackle, 8 to 12-pound test line, terminal tackle will be spinner baits, plastics, crankbaits and, for some, a popping cork over a live shrimp, you'll limit out every day on 4 to 15-pound Redfish. You'll be fishing the Atchafalaya Basin, the 'marsh', 30-miles wide and 90-miles long with most areas less than 6-feet deep. It's a nursery for Reds and it's full of bait, casting targets, grass flats, canals and creeks. From early March through the hot summer, the Gulf Coast Reds are a calling card for the weekend angler. See Theophile's website at www.neworleansfishing.com.

Fall! Oh, my goodness; 500 to 700 pounds of Redfish a day? Yessir! Georgia coast. Surprised? I was, but not now. Telephone Mark Noble, long time guide, local booster of fishing and St Simons Island native. He's the man, has spent his life fishing these waters and knows exactly when, where and how. You can come along. From September through November, in the shallow waters near the river mouths that flow into the bay, the Redfish gang up like I've never seen before and although you're gonna beef up your tackle a bit because the fish are so large, it's still sporting. The minimum length to keep a Red there is 27 inches. I've fished with Mark over a dozen times, caught probably over 6,000 pounds of Reds and never had one small enough to keep. I didn't mind. Maybe you should look up Mark at www.georgiafishing.net. It was some years ago that one of my sponsors staged what we called the 'Fishing Trip of a Lifetime' and a father and son from South Alabama won the trip. Sure enough, using three rods, one for me and one for each of them, we often caught three reds at a time with an average of 35 pounds. Think about that for a moment; over 100 pounds of beautiful Georgia Coast Reds at once. The photos of that trip are long since gone but we'll put up one or two more current ones to demonstrate the productivity you can expect when visiting Mark Noble.

O'Neill and Redfish in December

Winter! After reading this, I'll be expecting you to head to Pensacola Bay and Navarre Beach in December. Eddie Woodall is his name, and schooling Redfish is part of his game. I'm not sure exactly what happens, but it's something like this; when the river waters cool in December, it sends tons upon tons of bait down current into the bay. When this happens every year, hundreds of schools of Redfish, with thousands in each school, push the Poggies' to the surface. Low and behold, when the surface feeding birds give you the signal of activity, you'll motor over and begin casting and reeling large Road Runners tipped with plastics. Virtually every cast under the birds gets a hookup. When visiting Eddie the first time ever a couple of Decembers ago, he hyped it up a bit but did so in his soft voice so as not to get me too expectant. The birds indicated the first school and I hooked and caught a 20-pound Redfish on the first cast. After that stunning start, we caught and released at least 25 similar Reds before lunchtime. Think about that; 25 Reds over 20 pounds. That's 500 pounds. Eddie's site is www.fullnetfishingcharters.com.

So, why not give the good old dependable Redfish a chance and visit these fellows to make it complete?

Chapter 25: Carroll Lake Lodge

Camp on Carroll Lake

Have you tried it? If you haven't, do!

First of all, the destination for my little group was, has been most often, and probably will be always, www.carrolllakelodge.com. All you have to do is go to that site, leave a message and a fellow named Steve Brinkman will contact you and will handle everything from the time you land in Winnipeg. After that, a van will pick up your party and head for the floatplane. It's about a one-hour trip. You'll fly about 45-minutes to the lodge and start fishing that evening. You have to know that by the time you read this, you'll be making plans for next year along with me.

Where is it? Carroll Lake is six thousand pristine acres of clear water in the Woodland Caribou Provincial Park on the border between Ontario and Manitoba. The website will direct you as to the location in Canada.

When to go? I'll be there yearly in late May for four days and probably will be the first group visiting for the season. The lodge will be open from then until mid-September, about twelve weeks. I like it early. The ice has just broken up and the Northern Pike and Walleye are shallow and hungry. I have visited most often in middle to late August. Fishing is fabulous no matter when.

Who goes? The great thing about Carroll Lake Lodge, to me, is that it's small, exclusive (only your party of 8 or 10 can be there). It's doubtful that you will have to deal with strange people from

Pakistan or Russia or even California. The faulty personalities present for evening conversations and mealtime chatter will be the persons you recruit so you can't blame anyone but yourself if they are unpleasant and aggravating or maybe even liberals.

Travis with Respectable Walleye

What will you be catching? During the August or early September visits, using small 1/8th oz. Road Runners on light line fished in about 15 to 35-feet of water, you'll be catching Walleyes up to about 24 inches with most being 14 to 18 or so. If you insist on catching Walleyes in the 30-inch or over range, you can troll over the deep structure with large deep diving plugs, but that's incredibly boring and your boat partner will get tired of seeing you get hung up and likely losing the baits he has loaned to you. After getting the knack of it, you'll catch and release about 50 or so per day. For Northern Pike, you'll cast into the weedy coves around the grass and lily pads with a spinner bait (doesn't matter what color as long as it is chartreuse) or a weed-less spoon and plastic curly tail trailer. I like the spoons to be gold to kind of match the color of the little Perch that the carnivores feed on. Most of the Northern will be in the area of 22 to 28-inches with an occasional gangster topping 30 to 48 inches. Travis caught one last year at 48-inches, a real whopper for this far north. The Carroll Lake record is 50 inches. You and your boat mate will catch about 40 Pike per boat per ½ day. Let's figure that out for a moment. Say at 100 catches of Walleyes and Northern Pike per day for four days per 5 boats is 500 per day or over 2000 per trip. Is that to be enough?

Travis with Giant Northern Pike

What about if you visit early, say last week of May or first week of June? First of all, be notified that it'll be raining 80% of the time. It'll be a cool rain but the fishing's worth it. That time of the year, the lake is shallow and the Northern and Walleyes are caught in the little creeks. Travis and I located a little creek on the lodge map called "Moose Calf Creek." Who could pass up a creek named that, and it sounded good so we went there one morning. About a half mile up the creek was a huge beaver damn that stopped our travel. What the heck, make a cast or two. Travis and I caught 35 Northern Pike on 35 casts. If you go to Carroll Lake Lodge, you must find that place and catch a few.

Accommodations? There is a small cabin for two out on a little rocky point generally for husbands and wives, another larger coed spot atop a hill and then two lodges that can hold five guys each very comfortably. I suggest you keep your party at 8, or certainly no more than 10; accommodating 2, 2, 4 and 4 or 2, 2, 3 and 3 in each cabin as you desire. You'll be served breakfast each morning at 8AM, lunch will be fresh Walleye at 12:30PM and dinner at 6:30PM. You can have whatever you like, steaks, roasts, hamburgers, whatever, as a group. I suggest Walleye every day and every meal except breakfast. I mean, why not? Where I live and fish, Walleye is not accessible, so I eat it while I can. After the first meal, you'll vote for Walleye every meal also. There is no better game fish out of fresh water than Walleye. With un-hurried meals, it doesn't sound like you'll have enough fishing time. You will: before and after breakfast, after lunch, after dinner. See note above about 500 fish per day. Actually, I have to admit, we've had Walleye for breakfast too.

How to pack? Light outfits, jacket first for the mornings, rain suit is advisable for early in the year. Pack light though. Remember you'll be taking a float plane in with limited space. There is a washer and dryer there anyway if you need it. According to your instructions, Steve will import beer and adult beverages on the flights before you get there. I mean, really, you can't fish all the time and the beverages may spawn some outrageous stories. They are lies mostly, but they are fishing stories, so they are supposed be lies from the start.

Fishing gear? As you read this, take note, I'm a minimalist and will use as little as possible. Road Runners, Gold ½ ounce weedless spoons, and 100 curly tail plastics in white. You can use the plastics on the jigs and spoons. Two light action spinning rods wound with 6 or 8-pound mono, and two free spool reels and rods with 12 or 14-pound test.

Do you need a guide? No, you're on your own. If you're an angler at all, it shouldn't take you more than 30 minutes to figure it out. Again, see details about daily catches earlier in my note.

Don't forget the following gear, a couple of sets of pliers for each fisherman in the boat. You'll lose at least one set because of the Northern Pike's needle teeth. Bring along some heavy gauge mouth spreaders, and 12- inch sixty-pound test wire leaders for the Northern's toothy grin and a satellite phone just in case. Don't bring anything with treble hooks. You don't want to be digging out multi-hook baits from a big Northern Pike's spikey smile. Bring along some Bug Band bands, lotions and sprays. The mosquitos there are professionals. I say that, but using the Bug Band stuff, I've never been stung, not once.

What else do you need to know? Telephone my radio show at 800-wsb-talk on Saturday mornings from 4 to 6AM eastern and I'll tell you all about it. You can listen on the Internet or your phone or pad. Reread the column and contact Steve Brinkman at Carroll Lake on the web. He'll fix you up.

Chapter 26: Superlatives Easily Described: Best, Biggest, Most, Etc.

Darryl and Another Biggun'

You like superlative descriptions? I do; highest, fastest, biggest, easiest. Yes, indeed. I fished with the best Catfishing guide on the best Catfish lake, caught the biggest Catfish of my life, caught them faster than I ever thought, and finally caught the most pounds ever in one day.

Good Grief, tell me about this you say. I will. Read on!

Where? Santee Cooper Lakes, South Carolina. When? Most any month of the year including winter's coldest. With whom? Captain Darryl Smith working out of the Canal Lakes Fish Camp in Cross, South Carolina.

OK, here goes.

Captain Darryl has twenty-three line class world records, usually catches 300 to 500 pounds of catfish with his clients daily, out if his 30-foot pontoon boat, and has never, with me anyway, had any difficulty fulfilling his promises of a day to remember.

Darryl and Big Blue Cat

I have fished with Captain Darryl on five different occasions taping "O'Neill Outside" television shows. Each time, whether late winter, early spring, summer nights or clear fall days, we've swamped the pontoon with 30 to 60-pound Blue Cats. He targets the 'bigguns'. We fished deep structure, shallow lagoons and coves, bumped the old creek channel ledges and drifted the flats. During our most recent jaunt in December of '15, we caught numerous 6 to 10 pounders and topped off the short afternoon trip with double 35s. By the way, from the dock, fishing and back to the dock only takes about four hours. My cameraman, Jeff Alligood, and I drove from Atlanta, fished with Captain Darryl, and managed to return home before 10PM. For various reasons, that was necessary. You will want to stick around with Darryl and fish a day or two, at least.

Take a look at the photos accompanying this story. These were not always with me of course, but they chronicle Darryl's delivery with clients over the recent years.

Back to the superlatives; Darryl's biggest; 100.5 lbs. Blue Cat, the most; I'm guessing, but I'd say over 1,000 lbs. in a day; easiest, never takes more than a few hours if that is what you want, and all from an accessible fishery in South Carolina with cabins, lodges, a restaurant, ramp and a short run to the fishing grounds from Canal Lakes. Makes me want to go there again, and soon.

Santee Cooper Lakes, actually Lake Marion and Lake Moultrie, connected by a canal, total more than 180,000 acres. Let's think about that for a moment. Georgia's Lake Lanier at 37,000, Seminole at 34,000, Clarks Hill at 70,000 and finally Hartwell at 55,000, is about the same as total surface acres of Santee Cooper alone. It's hard to prove, of course, but the entire lake is paved on the bottom with healthy, sizeable, hungry catfish.

Darryl Smith

With Captain Darryl, you don't have to be an expert experienced angler, just watch the rod tips and when one, and often it's more than one at a time, tips toward the water, just start reeling. You will immediately feel the power of the big old whiskered rascals. It's a blast. Incidentally, the sixty-three pounder pictured was caught by a ten-year old. I'm sure he'll never forget it.

Take a look at the photos again and plan a trip to visit with Darryl this year. Look him up at www.captaindarryls.com and make a plan.

O'Neil with 167-Inch Whitetail Buck

Do you have a favorite fishing hat? In my days, I've worn all sorts of fishing hats. I'll bet you have too.

Around here I wear a fishing hat with various names on the front. Usually it's an O'Neill Outside logo. After all is said, advertising is everything. I buy them in bulk, so they don't cost much. I tell people that want one signed that the hat is worth about $6 before I sign it, and $3 afterward. They accept it anyway. The hats are thin and comfortable. However, my ears get sunburned and stay crusty all year long. I don't think that's good. Does that happen to you? I like hats though. When you have follicle challenges like I do, you tend to gravitate to hats. This challenge means I'm bald headed and have been since about the age of 23. Gail and I got married after I finished at Emory at age 21 and have been married over 53 years now. When she's not around, I blame it on her.

One of my grandfathers wore a straw hat when we were fishing in the small ponds around Loganville, Georgia about 63 years ago. I was 11; he was about 65. He was a primitive Baptist preacher and wore a starched white shirt and tie, black wingtip dress shoes, a vested black pinstriped suit and white gloves with the fingers cut out when we went to the local catfish ponds to catch a few. You'd think I'd have been embarrassed about that. I wasn't. I was just proud that he thought enough of me to take me fishing. My mother's father wore a fedora like Indiana Jones. When we walked to the river along the railroad tracks headed to the swift waters of the Tallulah River, we'd stop and drink the cold, clear spring waters flowing from the rocks. We'd tip the sweet drops from the brim of that old hat. Sure wish I had it now. I'd wear it. We used cane poles with black nylon line and red wigglers dug up from around the barn.

This was supposed to be a column about deer and deer hunting, so let's get to it and make it simple. I'm about to run out of room, so I'll be brief.

Whitetail deer are lazy critters that don't do much except, eat, sleep, look nervous, stay alive and are active only during the rut. That staying alive thing is a big deal, and they're good at it. Did I say sleep? It's not my kind of sleep, no sir. Thirty minutes at a time max, usually only five or 10, and sometimes with their eyes open. Ears are always alert and hyper wary. Can you sneak up on one while he's asleep? No, you can't. You think you can, but you can't. If he doesn't move and you think you're being extra sneaky, it's because he thinks he's hidden and you'll pass by. He knows you're there.

We are asked to include photos when we submit these columns so the one here is the largest Whitetail I ever took. He scored 167 inches. He was awake when I shot him.

Luther Turpin Age 45

Orphaned since he was ten, his two brothers and two sisters were sent to live with grandparents spread out across Rabun County in extreme northeast Georgia. His name was Luther Monroe Turpin and he was my maternal grandfather. Being the oldest of the five, he was portioned out to the least desirable destination, a moonshiner uncle who mistreated him, never seeing to any education of any type. He never went to school. He taught himself to read and write on his own. Stories handed down say that a large man, a 6'11" tall employee of his uncle, who bought his size 19 shoes from the Sears and Roebuck catalog, routinely disciplined him. This set of circumstances could be frightening for any ten-year-old.

Anyway, my grandfather ran away from that uncle when he was fourteen and worked in a logging camp along the Tallulah River. He recalled for me that day when he walked away saying that icicles were hanging off his hat and all his worldly possessions he carried in his coat pockets.

The tough, tall, rangy teenager, without a doubt much older acting and looking than his years, finally landed a job with the Tallulah Railroad, owned by Georgia Power, at $1 a day. He worked for Georgia Power his entire life until his retirement at sixty-five with a gold pocket-watch and a rod and reel as company gifts. Before retiring, he had become the locomotive driver or engineer. I used that rod and reel he received myself at about ten and, of course, wish I still had it. He was more comfortable with a long cane pole wound with black nylon line and a bucket of worms.

At seventeen, already having been totally on his own for three years, he noticed a young chestnut-haired girl, then thirteen, playing in a schoolyard in the small mountain community of Wiley, Georgia. It is said that he turned to a companion, asked her name and replied that she was the woman he would marry. The outlook for life was short in those days. You had to get on with it. Her name was Amanda Smith.

Mandy and Luther Turpin

They married two years later, produced seven children and had been together for fifty-two years when Mandy passed away at sixty-seven. Their third child and second girl was my mother, Margaret Fred Turpin. She was named for a favorite Uncle who was a Marine in the First World War.

Life in the North Georgia Mountains was surely hard. A garden and farm animals produced much needed food with so many mouths to feed, but cash money was scarce with such a brood. My mother relates that for one Christmas she got only an orange. Yes, an orange, and that was all, but it tasted good.

When I was about eight, Luther had retired and for a few weeks every summer, Luke and Mandy became my fishing buddies. We three visited Mandy's half sister and her family who had a little farm on the side of a mountain boarding the Tallulah River in Lakemont, Georgia. For our little fishing trips, we dug for worms behind the barn, carved out grubs from fallen pine trees along side of the hollows above the river, made a trap for crickets and I ranged around the fields catching grasshoppers. Once I sneaked off with my cousin and tried, at his insistence, some Brown's Mule Brand chewing tobacco. I got violently sick. They never said a word. Didn't have to I guessed. It has been over sixty-five years and I have not used tobacco since.

I vividly remember those quiet summer mornings in the mountains. We would walk along the railroad track between the rails, the three of us, with me in the middle. Those same rails my Grandfather had helped to spike into place 50-years before. It was two miles to the river. A steep descent took us to a deep pool beneath a trestle. It was on these warm days I came to know Luke and Mandy. They were life-long partners who shared all about their lives that a youngster, intent on the next bite, could absorb. We always walked back for lunch and Luke would slice fresh tomatoes with his pocketknife and make a sandwich for me on white bread. We would have peaches for desert.

A summer then was a grand prize waiting at the end of school. If I could relive a few weeks of any summer's fishing of all the worldwide trips I have taken, it would be with them, Luke and

Mandy, watching a small cork as it gently glides in the soft current of the Tallulah River hoping it would soon disappear.

Grandparents are, by and large, special people, and sometimes even fishing buddies. I just hope Gail and I are too after all is said and done. We are trying.

Elder Henry Nash

I wish you could have seen us; an attentive little boy with big ears and a stately old gentleman in a dark suit. What a team we made! I called him Granddaddy; he simply referred to me as "Son" and always with a smile. To everyone else he was Elder Nash, more about that in a moment.

My father was a pilot in the Army Air Corps and died in a plane crash when I was six-weeks old. My mother remarried when I was three and I not only got a fine man and war hero to be my father for sixtyy-eight years, I got a built-in fishing partner and Granddaddy. We fished for catfish, bass and bream in the small farm ponds in Walton, Rockdale and Gwinnett Counties in Georgia. Using worms, chicken livers, dough balls, just anything gathered up that might work, we generally made a formidable duo. The light line zipped from the little spinning reels we used zinging the baits as far into the ponds as we could and then, when the rods were mounted on forked sticks along the bank, we manned quite an arsenal.

What I remember most about him was his gentleness; never, and I mean never, raising his voice or declaring anything sterner than an occasional "Gee Whiz" when a sneaky little catfish stole his bait. But what a sight he was! Get this picture; black wing-tip shoes highly polished, dark charcoal grey pin-striped suit, starched white shirt and maroon and silver striped tie, white gloves, with the fingers cut out, all topped off with an expansive straw hat. He just did not like the sun. O'Neill was dressed in baggy jeans with 6-inch cuffs rolled up, a red, white and blue t-shirt and an Atlanta Cracker's baseball cap. I was a fan of the Crackers and would one day play shortstop in a series of high school championship games at the old Ponce de Leon Park, during which we won the state AAA title.

Many of the days we spent together on those ponds were quite productive. Seventy-five or more nice cats fell to our tactics. The pond owners always liked having Elder Nash visit. I guess it was a bit of payoff for his preaching to the congregations for free all those years. We didn't catch anything big you see, but that didn't matter. He was a bit over sixty and I was eleven. He was attentive to me and I was to him.

What about the Elder Nash part? Well, Henry Nash was an unpaid preacher to several Primitive Baptist congregations both in Atlanta and the various county churches. My father, mother and little brother that had come along when I was seven attended about once a month in the picturesque locations. Names of the churches like "Harris Springs", "Loganville", "Big Haynes Creek", and others come to mind. After the early morning service, we had dinner on the grounds; long tables covered with white cloths all spread out with delicacies. Some of the best food I have ever had came from those Christian women. It was usually warm and bright in my memory, Dogwoods dotted the forest with white delight and I knew Elder Nash and I would be fishing soon.

We spent dozens of fresh spring and warm, gentle summer days together, each being a treasured memory. From him I learned patience, and the positive effect of soft words. More than anything, I remember his quiet reserve and his love for all things. I wish I could see him again. I'll bet we could still catch'em.

Chapter 30: The Road Ahead

Editor's note: With much credit and respect given to O'Neill's most favorite outdoor writer and storyteller, Tom Kelly, we include the final chapter from "A FORK IN THE ROAD" by Tom Kelly Inc. www.tomkellyinc.net

We have said nearly enough, and I'm sure that for some of you it has been more than enough, but we have been dealing with a complicated subject rather than one that has a few simple rules that can be easily explained.

If there is a single, overriding trait that a turkey has, it is the fact of his everlasting unpredictability. Next to this trait everything else fades into insignificance.

As you go down this new road you have chosen, you are going to find very few turkeys that are alike. What worked once might not work next time. Actions that ran one off this time might bring one right into your lap next time.

What you have undertaken to try to do is to convince a bird that is suspicious by nature, whose eyesight is superb, whose sense of hearing is impressive, and whose native caution has to be experienced to be appreciated, to drop whatever he has been doing and come within fifty yards of where you sit, by the use of a single one of his senses, that of hearing.

Sight is of no use to you, except in the case of decoys on the edge of a pasture, and occasionally the very sight of these decoys will cause him to stop, go into what the book calls display, and expect the hen he has heard, and now believes he sees, to come to him.

Except in the rarest of instances, you must depend upon him to advertise his location when he gobbles or yelps, which means that he must be the one who opens the action. After the action opens the continuation of the affair will be conducted almost wholly by means of the sense of sound. So not only is he the one who originates the contact, it is up to him to maintain it, and he can be induced to do so only by sounds you make, sounds that cause him to respond.

You have five senses and he has only four, because he lacks the sense of smell. But since your sense of smell is so imperfectly developed, for the purpose of a turkey hunt you have only the same four that he does.

In hunting him, the two of you are even more equal than that because no matter how many senses each of you has and/or uses, the hunt is conducted almost wholly by sound, until right at the final moment, when you decide whether or not to pull the trigger.

You are going to find him endlessly fascinating, occasionally easy, regularly difficult, and frequently impossible, but never dull.

Two quick examples will help me make that point.

I know a man who called up and killed his first turkey the year I was born. He is still alive, is still moderately active, and he hunted several times this past season. He called and invited me to go with him the last weekend of the season, but I could not, because of prior commitments. He had at that time killed one and missed one.

Thin seasons happen to the best of us, no matter what level of experience we may enjoy.

Example number two is a man who is no longer with us, but he was a man who began hunting turkeys in 1915 and hunted them until he got to the age of 90. By the time he was 85 he had grown as deaf as a post, had to have a family retainer along to pull his sleeve and point out the direction of sounds to him, and he needed a little help to carry the tools of the hunt into the woods. But he continued to do his own calling, was absolutely in control of his own hunts and brought home a turkey every once in a while as well.

At the age of 85 he was the first man to leave the camp house before daylight, the last one in at lunch, the first one back after midday, and the last one back after sundown. I was told, and I believe it, that when he was a broth of a boy of 75, he carried a lunch and a canteen of water and stayed in the woods until dark. Lunch breaks, in his opinion, were the mark of the dilettante.

Any creature that can inspire that level of enthusiasm in intelligent people, and maintain it for that long a period of years, has progressed a long way beyond respect. He has crossed over the threshold and is occupying a position of reverence.

In my own case, while I have noted that the length of service of either of these two paragons, I have been at this for a very long time.

There isn't now, and never has been any diminution in the degree of interest with which I approach the hunt. There have been some physical changes.

Years ago, I crossed foot logs with the same speed and gait with which I traversed level sidewalks. I cross them yet, but if you were there the sight of it would remind you of those ancient woodcuts of the French tightrope walker midway in his crossing of Niagara Falls in the 1890s. I can still get over foot logs but the last adjective that would come to your mind if you were present at the event would be the word quick.

I have not heard a turkey drum for the last three or four years. At best, I never could hear it beyond 75 or 80 yards, never could course the sound properly, and it always seemed to me that I felt it in the pit of my stomach, rather than hearing it.

Turkeys, of course, have not stopped drumming; I have simply stopped hearing them. I am in the position of the man who took a series of golf lessons, found that his ability to hit fairway woods had improved to the extent that he could hit them out of sight, and was delighted with his progress until he discovered that what he really needed was to have his glasses changed.

I shot a turkey across a waist-deep creek, thirty feet wide, some two years ago. After he quit flopping I undressed and waded across to effect the retrieve. It seemed to me that the water was a touch colder than it had been twenty years ago but it may have been the weather.

But all of these, and one or two others, are simply the flow of water that smoothes the stone.

The fascination remains, the anticipation is unchanged, and the deep satisfaction when a turkey does something you expected him to do is no less comforting. The level of surprise, when a turkey does something outside of your experience, and makes you feel as if you had a room temperature IQ, is no less painful.

I may be fooled less, but I am still fooled often and badly, and any man, no matter what his level of experience, who tells you that he is never surprised and never out-thought, is being extremely reckless with the truth.

What I have tried to do in these pages is to give you some idea of the basics. The subject is far too complicated and intellectually challenging to be able to be reduced to a series of principles, which if memorized and followed would guarantee success. The millions of subtleties you can expect to encounter will have to be dealt with, individually, at the time they arise.

You couldn't be coming along at a better time.

The way you get proficient at this business is by making stupid mistakes in front of turkeys, turkeys that delight in pointing out these errors to you as they walk away in the opposite direction. Walk away for reasons for which you have no clue.

The times are so much better than they used to be because there are so many more turkeys to be stupid in front of.

Professions and Thank You Praises

Quite often, when being approached by outdoorsmen, fishermen, hunters, and people who watch the television program or listen to the radio in which I am involved, I get a bit embarrassed by the praise. No do not get me wrong, I enjoy it. Who would not? Lately, however, I have taken a look at what I do for a living and how I feel about it. Stick with me for a moment on this.

I enjoy what I do and support my family by doing it. Good. But is it worthy of exaggerated praise? Maybe I do not feel worthy. Have I got people fooled? Maybe!

I will get to the point. I do not want the attention, being recognized, congratulated for entertaining and informative programs to end, but I think that it is more appropriate for workers in other professions to be praised, such as; teachers, policemen, firemen, nurses, doctors, medical researchers, volunteer hospital and mental health center workers.

You see, in recent years, I have had a loved one cured of a life-threatening illness because of intelligent, dedicated, hardworking people who have learned about how to treat and cure deadly diseases. I have seen and heard of policemen and firemen who risked their lives to both protect and save the lives of citizens they had never met. I know of teachers who spend long, personal, attentive hours to go the extra mile so that some young person can realize the joy and fulfillment of the learning experience.

So, if you see me at the airport, in a restaurant, or sports show, on the lake, be sure to say hello, and if it is the case, tell me how you enjoy our shows and what you may have learned. I will welcome it. But too, when you see a policeman, fireman, teacher, doctor, or nurse, you might consider saying thank you to them too. I will.

The History of Big Green Egg Throughout Civilization

In the beginning there was wood, dry leaves, lightning and eventually, fire. Early man soon learned about the flavor benefits of cooking meat over this exciting discovery, which quickly gained acclaim as far superior to gnawing on raw Tyrannosaurus ribs! Eventually, specialties such as smoked brie and s'mores were added to their culinary repertoire!

Later cultures discovered that the results were even better when the fire and food were contained inside a dome-shaped, earthen vessel. Evidence of these early prototypes of the Big Green Egg have been found by archeologists in the ruins of nearly every civilization around the world ... except the Propanians, who preferred to scorch their meals using volcanic gasses, and the DriveThruians, who ate all their meals from take-out and quickly vanished from planet earth.

Today's Big Green Egg is a modern-day evolution of these ancient cookers. Its design is modeled on the clay cooking vessels first seen during the Chinese Qin Dynasty and then used by the Japanese beginning in the 3rd century. Centuries ago, these knee-high cookers were fueled by wood or natural charcoal (just like the Big Green Egg is today), and pots were hung inside them for cooking rice. Eventually a slatted cooking grid was fitted inside for grilling and roasting meats, and by the 1600s they were raised off the floor and placed on a platform – a position which undoubtedly was much easier on the cook's back!

Popularity began to spread as U.S. servicemen discovered this type of cooker during World War II and shipped them home after the war. The domed cookers were an exciting alternative to the metal charcoal or gas grills of the day, and people became enamored with the added flavor and juiciness this "newly discovered" style of cooking gave to foods.

American serviceman and entrepreneur Ed Fisher was one of those guys who discovered the domed clay cooker while overseas. He was amazed at how much better the food tasted, and he began to import them sensing that there might be an interest back home. When Ed opened the first Big Green Egg store in Atlanta in 1974, he sold a simple clay cooker based on the same design and materials that had been used thousands of years ago. Despite the great results they produced, these original cookers were fragile and not durable after exposure to the elements.

Ed Fisher was fully committed to developing a company to produce and market these amazing cookers, and set out to make the best one that had ever been created.

As his efforts gained popularity, he made the decision to refine the composition of the EGG and aligned the company with a state-of-the-art factory to manufacture his products in the hands of skilled ceramic artisans. Company engineers incorporated new types of ceramics, based on materials initially developed by NASA for the space program, and worked tirelessly to find ways to improve the design. The result was a far superior cooker that is stronger, more durable and provides better heat insulation than anything else on the market, a distinction the Big Green Egg is known for today.

From Ed's original Big Green Egg, the product line has grown to include seven sizes of the EGG available throughout the world in over fifty countries, with hundreds of accessories designed to make cooking just about anything on a Big Green Egg fun, entertaining and delicious!

Often copied, but never equaled - the Big Green Egg is the Ultimate Cooking Experience!

Succulent Selections Prepared on a Big Green Egg

Shrimp Stuffed Jalapenos

Shrimp Stuffed Jalapenos

Ingredients

- 8 jalapenos
- 4 ounces of cream cheese
- 16 medium shrimp
- 1 lb bacon
- Old Bay Seasoning to taste

Method

- Set the EGG for indirect cooking with the convEGGtor at 400°F.
- Remove the stems and split the jalapenos in half lengthwise. Carefully cut out the vein in the jalapeno and remove the seeds. Place the jalapeno halves in a strainer and rinse thoroughly.
- Fill the peppers with cream cheese. Remove the tail of the shrimp and place a single shrimp on the jalapeno. Wrap each jalapeno with a slice of bacon and set into a baking dish. Sprinkle with Old Bay Seasoning.
- Place the jalapenos on the EGG for 15 minutes, turning them half way through.
- When the bacon is browned, remove the pan from the EGG and let stand for 4 to 5 minutes before serving.

Fish Chowder

Fish Chowder

Ingredients

- 4 cups grilled crappie or white fish
- ½ pound bacon
- 1 cup flour
- 1 large onion chopped
- 2 cups chicken broth
- 1 bottle clam juice
- 6 potatoes, cubed
- ½ gallon half and half
- Salt and pepper to taste

Method

- Set the EGG for direct cooking without the convEGGtor at 350°F.
- Season fish with salt and pepper, place on a perforated grid and cook until the fish flakes easily. Remove from the EGG and break into bite-sized pieces.
- In a Dutch oven, fry bacon until crisp, then break into small pieces. Add onions and cook until soft. Add flour to pan with bacon and drippings to make a roux. Add chicken broth, clam juice and stir until mixed. Add potatoes cook until tender.
- Add half and half and salt and pepper to taste. Cook for about 20 minutes, then add the fish. If you like a thicker chowder, add a little cornstarch mixed with water. Stir and cook additional 5 minutes.
- This chowder is wonderful served in a bowl or hollowed out round bread loaf.

Crab Stuffed Whitefish

Crab Stuffed Whitefish

Ingredients

- 1 Tbsp olive oil
- ½ cup onion chopped
- 2 cloves garlic minced
- 1 cup crabmeat, chopped
- 2 Tbsp cream cheese
- ½ to 1 tsp Old Bay Seasoning
- Salt and pepper to taste
- 2 Tbsp garlic chives, chopped
- 2 lbs white fish filets
- Old Bay Seasoning

Lemon Butter Sauce

- 2 Tbsp butter
- Juice of 1 lemon

Method

- Set the EGG for direct cooking without the convEGGtor at 350°F.
- In a Stir Fry & Paella Pan, add the olive oil and heat. Add onions and cook until they begin to caramelize then add garlic. Add crabmeat, cream cheese, Old Bay Seasoning, salt and pepper and chives. Stir well; remove from heat and allow to cool.
- Spread the crabmeat mixture onto the fish filets. Roll up each fish fillet and place seam side down on a perforated cooking grid.
- In a cast iron sauce pan, melt butter and add the lemon juice, Old Bay Seasoning and salt and pepper. Brush over fish.
- Place the perforated grid in the EGG and cook for about 25 minutes or until fish flakes easily.

Cajun Shrimp Burgers

Cajun Shrimp Burgers

Ingredients

- 1½ lbs raw shrimp, peeled and deveined
- 4 Tbsp olive oil or coconut oil, divided
- 1 small shallot, finely minced
- 1 clove garlic, finely minced
- ¼ cup yellow or red pepper, finely minced
- 1 tsp sea salt
- ½ tsp pepper
- 1 tsp chili powder
- 1 tsp paprika
- 1 tsp cayenne pepper
- 1 tsp Dijon mustard
- 1 tsp lemon juice
- 1 Tbsp Worcestershire sauce
- 1 large egg, beaten

Cajun Mustard

- 1 green onion chopped
- ¾ cup coconut cream or mayonnaise
- 1 Tbsp Dijon mustard
- 1 Tbsp ketchup
- 1 tsp Worcestershire sauce
- 1 tsp horseradish
- 1 tsp paprika
- 1 tsp lemon juice
- ½ tsp cayenne pepper
- ½ tsp chili powder
- ½ teaspoon salt

Method

- Set the EGG for direct cooking without the convEGGtor at 425°F.
- Add shrimp to your food processor and pulse until the mixture is in small pieces. Remove and place into a mixing bowl.
- In a Stir Fry & Paella Pan, heat 1 tablespoon oil. Add shallot, garlic, and peppers, cook for about 4 minutes until softened. Season with salt and pepper. Remove from heat and let cool.

• Add the remaining ingredients and cooled pepper mixture to shrimp bowl and stir to combine. Mold to your desired burger size and refrigerate for 30 minutes.

• In a small bowl, combine Cajun Mustard ingredients and set aside.

• Cook the burgers on a cast iron grid for 3 to 4 minutes per side until golden brown and cooked through.

Surf and Turf Kabobs

Surf and Turf Kabobs

Ingredients

- 1 clove garlic, minced
- 4 tsp butter
- 1 Tbsp olive oil
- 1 tsp lemon zest
- ¼ cup fresh tarragon, chopped
- Salt and pepper to taste
- 1 lb. rib-eye steak
- 1 lb. peeled and deveined shrimp

Method

- Set the EGG for direct cooking at 450°F.
- Mix garlic with butter, olive oil and lemon zest. Heat in a cast iron sauce pot just long enough to melt butter. Stir in tarragon, salt, and pepper. Set aside
- Cut the ribeye into cubes about ¾ inch square. Thread the beef onto flexible skewer; thread shrimp onto an additional skewer. Place beef skewer on the cooking grid; add the shrimp skewer about 4 minutes after the beef. Cook to desired degree of doneness.
- Remove skewers and brush liberally with the butter sauce. To serve, divide beef and shrimp evenly.

Fish Pot Pie

Fish Pot Pie

Ingredients

- Several pounds of cubed redfish
- Potatoes
- Green Beans
- Carrots
- Onions
- Cream of Mushroom soup
- French fried onions
- 1 roll of crescent roll dough
- one large can of Vegall vegetables

Method

- Set the EGG for indirect cooking with the convEGGtor at 400°F.
- In a Dutch oven, add the green beans, potatoes, carrots and onions; cover with water and place on the cooking grid and boil until the potatoes and carrots are soft. Remove and drain.
- Place cubes of redfish in the Dutch oven. Add the drained boiled vegetables onto the fish. Pour the cream of mushroom soup and spread across the top of the vegetables. Layer on the fried onions.
- Roll out crescent roll dough and lay it on top of the other ingredients in the pan.
- Place the Dutch oven back in the EGG and bake for 30-40 minutes.

Bass with Brown Butter and Capers

Bass with Brown Butter and Capers

Ingredients

- 1 cup flour
- 1 Tbsp black pepper
- 1 Tbsp white pepper
- 1 Tbsp cayenne pepper
- 2 Tbsp kosher salt
- 4 bass fillets
- 6 Tbsp butter, divided
- ¼ cup capers
- Juice of 1 lemon
- ½ cup white wine

Method

- Set the EGG for direct cooking without the convEGGtor at 400°F.
- Combine flour, peppers and salt. Dredge fish fillets in flour mixture and shake off any excess.
- Melt 2 tablespoons of butter in the cast iron skillet. Heat until butter is brown but not burned. Place fish in the skillet and sauté 3-4 minutes on each side.
- Remove the fish from the skillet and wipe out excess butter. Add capers, lemon juice and wine. Cook for 5 minutes and then add the remaining 4 tablespoons of butter. Stir to blend, then, ladle the sauce over the fish.

Spicy Soy-Ginger Grilled Striped Bass with Asparagus

Spicy Soy-Ginger Grilled Striped Bass with Asparagus

Ingredients

- 2 Tbsp reduced sodium soy sauce
- 2 Tbsp lemon juice, divided
- 1½ tsp sugar
- 1½ tsp fresh ginger, minced
- 1½ tsp powdered ginger
- ½ tsp red pepper flakes
- ¼ cup canola oil
- 1 bunch (about 1 pound) asparagus, bottom halves trimmed and saved for another use
- ¾ lb striped bass or other white fish cut into 6 2oz portions Kosher salt and black pepper
- 1 Tbsp extra virgin olive oil

Method

- Prepare EGG for direct heat at 450°F with a cast iron grid, flat side up.
- In a blender combine soy sauce, 1 tablespoon lemon juice, sugar, fresh and powdered ginger and red pepper flakes. Blend to combine. With blender running slowly pour in canola oil and continue to mix for 30 seconds.
- Spread asparagus on a rimmed pan, pour half of the soy sauce mixture over the asparagus and toss to coat. Reserve remaining marinade.
- Rinse fish and pat dry. Season both sides with salt and pepper and drizzle with olive oil and remaining lemon juice.
- Place the fish skin side down on the grid. Cook for 3 minutes; flip and grill 3 more minutes. At the same time, grill asparagus turning once or twice until tender and brown. Divide.

Grilled Bass with Pecan Herb Crust

Grilled Bass with Pecan Herb Crust

Ingredients

- 4 Tbsp champagne vinegar or white wine vinegar
- 1 Tbsp Dijon mustard
- 2 tsp prepared horseradish
- 1 Tbsp mayonnaise
- 2 Tbsp olive oil
- 4 bass fillets
- ½ cup pecans, finely chopped
- 2 cloves garlic, minced
- 2 Tbsp fresh mined tarragon
- 2 Tbsp minced Italian parsley
- 1 Tbsp lemon zest (or ½ Tbsp each of lemon and orange zest)

Method

- Set the EGG for direct cooking with a Cast Iron Grid (flat side up) at 500°F. Soak hickory chips for smoking.
- Combine vinegar, mustard, horseradish, mayonnaise and olive oil in a large bowl. Add fish and coat well; leave the fish in the mixture to marinate for one hour.
- Combine pecans, garlic, herbs and zest in a shallow baking dish. Shake the from the fish, and dredge the fish in the pecan mixture, pressing nuts onto the fish to coat evenly.
- Place the fish directly on grid in a single layer; close the dome and cook about 3 minutes. Turn the fish and cook another 5-7 minutes. Remove from grid and garnish with lemon wedges and sprigs of herbs.

Striped Bass Fish Tacos

Striped Bass Fish Tacos

- 3 cups diced tomatoes
- 1 small Serrano chile, stemmed, seeded and minced
- 1 Tablespoon minced shallot
- 2 Tablespoons finely chopped cilantro
- Juice of 2 limes
- Sea Salt
- 2 Tablespoons extra virgin olive oil
- 1 pound skinless striped bass
- 8 6-inch corn tortillas
- 1 avocado halved seeded and diced
- 1 lime cut into wedges for serving

Method

- In a medium bowl, combine tomatoes with the chili, shallot, cilantro, and lime juice. Season with salt and let the salsa stand for 10 minutes stirring occasionally.
- In paella pan, heat olive oil. Season fish with sea salt and add it to the pan. Grill over high heat until browned, 6 minutes.
- Warm tortillas, transfer fish to tortillas and top with salsa and avocado.

Sriracha Brown Sugar Shrimp

Sriracha Brown Sugar Shrimp

- 2 Tablespoons brown sugar
- 1 ½ Tablespoons sriracha sauce
- 1 Tablespoon olive oil
- Salt and pepper to taste
- 1 clove garlic finely minced
- ½ pound peeled and deveined shrimp with tails left on
- 1 Tablespoon chopped chives

Method

- In a small bowl, stir brown sugar, sriracha, oil, salt, pepper, and garlic together.
- Toss with shrimp to marinate about 30 minutes. Skewer onto kebob sticks and grill about 3 minutes per side or until completely opaque.
- Remove from grill and sprinkle with chopped chives.

Grilled Oysters with Habanero Butter

Grilled Oysters with Habanero Butter

- 2 sticks unsalted butter, softened
- 2 Tablespoons El Yucateo Green Habanero hot sauce
- 2 Tablespoons chopped parsley
- ½ teaspoon kosher salt
- ¼ teaspoon freshly ground pepper
- 3 dozen medium to large oysters

Method

- Stir together the softened butter, habanero sauce, salt and pepper until well combined.
- Transfer the butter mixture to a sheet of plastic wrap and roll into a 2 inch log. Refrigerate until the butter has firmed up, about 15 minutes. Slice the butter into 36 pats.
- Place oysters on the hot grill flat side up. Cover the grill and cook until the oysters open, about 5 minutes and loosed the oysters from the bottom of the shells, being careful to keep the liquid inside the shell.
- Remove the top shells and loosed the oysters from the bottom shell. Top each oyster with a pat of habanero butter and return the oysters to the grill.
- Cover the grill and cook until the butter is mostly melted and the oysters are hot. About 1 minute.

Grilled Walleye with Mango Salsa

Grilled Walleye with Mango Salsa

For the walleye

- 1 large walleye fillet
- 1 Tablespoon olive oil
- Salt and pepper to taste

For the Mango Salsa

- 1 large mango, cubed
- 1 large tomato chopped
- 2 Tablespoons red onion, diced
- 1 Tablespoon cilantro, minced
- 1 Tablespoon lime juice

Method

- Preheat grill to 400 degrees.
- Combine all ingredients for the mango salsa in a medium sized bowl. Stir to incorporate. Refrigerate until ready to serve.
- Rub olive oil all over the walleye fillet and sprinkle the flesh side with salt and pepper.
- Place walleye fillet on the grill skin side down. Cook for 8-10 minutes flipping half way through.
- Serve with skin side down and garnish with mango salsa.

Made in the USA
Columbia, SC
10 March 2021